910.45   Yount, Lisa.

YOU   Pirates

Pirates

Other Books in the History Makers Series:

Pirates

By Lisa Yount

LUCENT BOOKS
SAN DIEGO, CALIFORNIA

Detroit • New York • San Diego • San Francisco
Boston • New Haven, Conn. • Waterville, Maine
London • Munich

To Captain Sis, Mrs. Mac, and Karen in salute to our pirate dreams

Library of Congress Cataloging-in-Publication Data

Yount, Lisa.
  Pirates / by Lisa Yount.
    p.   cm. — (History makers)
Includes bibliographical references (p.) and index.
  ISBN 1-56006-955-4 (hardback : alk. paper)
  1. Pirates—Juvenile literature. [1. Pirates.] I. Title. II. Series.
  G535 .Y68 2002
  910.4'5—dc21

2001006269

Copyright 2002 by Lucent Books,
an imprint of The Gale Group
10911 Technology Place, San Diego, California 92127

Printed in the U.S.A.

CONTENTS

FOREWORD

The literary form most often referred to as "multiple biography" was perfected in the first century A.D. by Plutarch, a perceptive and talented moralist and historian who hailed from the small town of Chaeronea in central Greece. His most famous work, *Parallel Lives*, consists of a long series of biographies of noteworthy ancient Greek and Roman statesmen and military leaders. Frequently, Plutarch compares a famous Greek to a famous Roman, pointing out similarities in personality and achievements. These expertly constructed and very readable tracts provided later historians and others, including playwrights like Shakespeare, with priceless information about prominent ancient personages and also inspired new generations of writers to tackle the multiple biography genre.

The Lucent History Makers series proudly carries on the venerable tradition handed down from Plutarch. Each volume in the series consists of a set of five to eight biographies of important and influential historical figures who were linked together by a common factor. In *Rulers of Ancient Rome*, for example, all the figures were generals, consuls, or emperors of either the Roman Republic or Empire; while the subjects of *Fighters Against American Slavery*, though they lived in different places and times, all shared the same goal, namely the eradication of human servitude. Mindful that politicians and military leaders are not (and never have been) the only people who shape the course of history, the editors of the series have also included representatives from a wide range of endeavors, including scientists, artists, writers, philosophers, religious leaders, and sports figures.

Each book is intended to give a range of figures—some well known, others less known; some who made a great impact on history, others who made only a small impact. For instance, by making Columbus's initial voyage possible, Spain's Queen Isabella I, featured in *Women Leaders of Nations*, helped to open up the New World to exploration and exploitation by the European powers. Inarguably, therefore, she made a major contribution to a series of events that had momentous consequences for the entire world. By contrast, Catherine II, the eighteenth-century Russian queen, and Golda Meir, the modern Israeli prime minister, did not play roles of global impact; however, their policies and actions significantly influenced the historical development of both their own countries and their regional neighbors. Regardless of their relative importance in the greater historical scheme, all of the figures chronicled in the History Makers series made contributions to posterity; and their public achievements, as well as what is known about their private lives, are presented and evaluated in light of the most recent scholarship.

In addition, each volume in the series is documented and substantiated by a wide array of primary and secondary source quotations. The primary source quotes enliven the text by presenting eyewitness views of the times and culture in which each history maker lived; while the secondary source quotes, taken from the works of respected modern scholars, offer expert elaboration and/ or critical commentary. Each quote is footnoted, demonstrating to the reader exactly where biographers find their information. The footnotes also provide the reader with the means of conducting additional research. Finally, to further guide and illuminate readers, each volume in the series features photographs, two bibliographies, and a comprehensive index.

The History Makers series provides both students engaged in research and more casual readers with informative, enlightening, and entertaining overviews of individuals from a variety of circumstances, professions, and backgrounds. No doubt all of them, whether loved or hated, benevolent or cruel, constructive or destructive, will remain endlessly fascinating to each new generation seeking to identify the forces that shaped their world.

Adventurous Lives

At most costume parties, some guests dress as modern-day figures such as astronauts. Others imitate adventurous characters from the past. Among these—the cowboys and cowgirls, Queen Elizabeths, and Robin Hoods—there are likely to be some pirates. Complete with an eye patch, a broad-brimmed hat with a feather plume, a fake cutlass, and perhaps even a plastic parrot or a black flag bearing a skull and crossbones, a pirate costume makes a striking outfit.

Costume designers and wearers alike probably draw their mental pictures of pirates from novels such as Robert Louis Stevenson's *Treasure Island,* movies or television shows about pirates, or children's stories in which pirates are comic villains. These sources have made many people believe that pirates led a romantic, exciting life, free of all the social rules that bind ordinary individuals. The same depictions may make others wonder whether pirates ever existed outside of writers' vivid imaginations.

The Real Pirates

Many of the book and movie images of pirates are wrong. Few, if any, pirates buried hoards of treasure or made their victims walk the plank, for instance. Still, pirates were real—and, especially for about fifty years in the late seventeenth and early eighteenth centuries, they played an important part in history. Their criminal activities had powerful effects on the growing trade between Europe and the Americas, India, and Africa. Attempts to end those activities made European nations rethink the ways they used their navies and governed their colonies in distant parts of the world.

Among the pirates who swept the seas at that key time, a handful of leaders gained fame that has lasted far beyond their own day. Some, like William Dampier and Woodes Rogers, wrote books about their adventures, based on detailed diaries that they had kept during their travels. Others attracted the attention of writers who produced popular accounts of their lives. Thanks to these accounts, names like Henry Morgan and Bartholomew Roberts, Blackbeard and Captain William Kidd, still stir feelings of admiration mixed with horror.

These men—and a few women, too, such as Anne Bonny—are the realities on which later writers' fictional pirates were based. A look at what is known of their lives and careers gives a clearer picture of a pirate's daily existence than any novel. It also shows the variety of personalities who were attracted to this exciting but risky way of life. They range from Dampier, who was as much a scientist as an adventurer, to Edward Teach (Blackbeard), who made his impression on history mostly through his reputation for terror.

Some of these famous leaders, such as "Black Bart" Roberts, were very successful in their chosen work. Others, such as Morgan and Rogers, mixed at times with well-to-do society and held high political posts. At the opposite extreme were William Kidd and Anne Bonny, who owed their fame—and fatal downfall—mostly to having been in the wrong place at the wrong time. But as different as these people were in luck and personality, they all possessed the mixture of ruthlessness and courage, self-discipline and love of freedom, that has made pirates, both real and fictional, fascinating figures to this day.

The Pirates' Golden Age

Piracy is nothing more than armed robbery on the ocean. It has no doubt existed ever since human beings began sailing and trading at sea. Ancient Greek and Roman writings mentioned pirates, and pirates are still at work today. The most famous pirates of all time, however—the ones most people think of when they hear the word *pirate*—operated in the Caribbean Sea, off the coasts of Africa, and in the Atlantic Ocean off southeastern North America between about 1665 and 1725. Some historians have called this period the golden age of piracy.

The Buccaneers

The first pirates of the golden age were descended from ragged bands of refugees, unemployed sailors, runaway servants and slaves, and petty criminals united mainly by their hatred of Spain. In the early 1600s, these groups had lived in the forested interior of the large island of Hispaniola, which today contains the countries of Haiti and the Dominican Republic. They hunted wild pigs and cattle, the remains of herds abandoned by earlier Spanish settlers, and sold the animals' meat and hides to passing ships. They smoke-dried the meat on wooden grills that the native Arawaks who had invented them called *buccans*. The hunters therefore came to be known as buccaneers.

The Spanish drove the hunters out of Hispaniola's forests in the 1630s. Many of the refugees moved to a smaller island just off Hispaniola's northwestern coast, named Tortuga because it was shaped like a turtle. Spanish ships laden with valuable goods had to pass through a narrow strait near Tortuga, and the displaced hunters soon began to seize these tempting vessels. So many of the buccaneers turned to piracy that by the 1660s, *buccaneer* had become more or less a synonym for *pirate*. The buccaneer bands grew large enough to have major effects on trade in the Caribbean Sea, and the golden age of piracy began.

By that time, Tortuga was not the only pirate base in the Caribbean. After the British took Jamaica from Spain in 1655, the island's governors encouraged buccaneers such as Henry Morgan to establish themselves in Port Royal, a city on a sand spit outside a large bay on Jamaica's southern coast. "With a vast harbor capable of sheltering five hundred ships, an ideal location at the center of Caribbean shipping routes, a ready market, and sympathetic officials, Port Royal was pirate heaven,"[1] historian Jenifer G. Marx has written. Some people called Port Royal the wickedest city in the world.

Pirates and Privateers

Wicked or not, the activities of some buccaneers—and later sea rovers of the golden age as well—were more or less legal. This was because piracy overlapped an accepted war tactic of the time called privateering. European nations and their colonies added to the strength of their limited navies by authorizing privately owned ships to attack the merchant ships of the countries they were fighting. These licensed ships, as well as the sailors who worked on them, were called privateers. English, French, and Dutch colonies in the Caribbean often licensed buccaneers to be privateers against Spain, for instance. Privateers were paid by being allowed to keep most of the cargoes of the ships they seized.

The licenses that gave privateers permission to seize certain ships were called letters of marque. As long as privateers captured only ships owned by the nations listed in their letters of marque, they were not

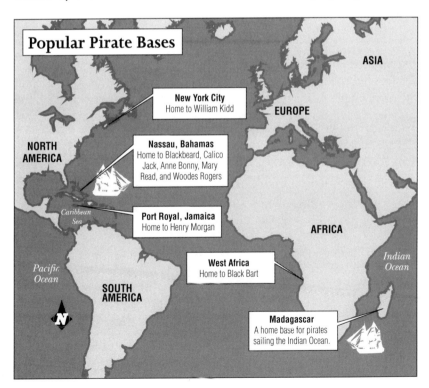

Popular Pirate Bases

ASIA

EUROPE

New York City
Home to William Kidd

NORTH AMERICA

Nassau, Bahamas
Home to Blackbeard, Calico Jack, Anne Bonny, Mary Read, and Woodes Rogers

Caribbean Sea

Port Royal, Jamaica
Home to Henry Morgan

AFRICA

Pacific Ocean

West Africa
Home to Black Bart

Indian Ocean

SOUTH AMERICA

Madagascar
A home base for pirates sailing the Indian Ocean.

pirates. In reality, however, the line between privateering and piracy was often blurred. The buccaneer Henry Morgan, for instance, carried letters of marque from the governor of Jamaica permitting him to attack Spanish ships and cities, which made him a privateer. However, the governor had the right to issue such documents only as long as Jamaica's mother country, England, was at war with Spain. The two countries signed a peace treaty just before one of Morgan's biggest raids. Therefore, Morgan technically was a pirate during this raid. Many "pirate" leaders of the golden age, from Morgan to Woodes Rogers, were privateers for at least part of their careers.

The Red Sea Men

The first wave of golden age piracy, the era of the buccaneers, ebbed away after England and Spain signed a peace treaty in 1670, making British privateer attacks on Spanish ships and ports illegal. In 1693, however, pirates recognized a new opportunity when a band of raiders led by an American, Thomas Tew, captured a ship in the Indian Ocean carrying treasure as fabulous as that of Spanish galleons that had attracted the buccaneers.

Often bankrolled by merchants in New York, Philadelphia, or Boston, sea rovers swarmed to the Indian Ocean and Red Sea to seize other heavily laden ships sailing between India and the Middle East.

Pirates load the stolen booty from a Spanish galleon aboard their ship.

They created shantytowns on and near the large island of Madagascar, off Africa's east coast. These pirates, sometimes termed the "Red Sea men," traveled between the American colonies and the Madagascar settlements in a yearly commute that came to be called the Pirate Round. Piracy in the Indian Ocean remained profitable until the start of the eighteenth century, when the powerful British East India Company, determined to maintain good trade relations with India, persuaded Britain to send more warships to the area.

The Final Wave

The third and largest wave of piracy during the golden age began in 1713, when a long war in Europe came to an end. The declaration of peace left thousands of navy and privateer sailors unemployed. The governor of Jamaica warned officials in London:

> Since the calling in of our privateers, I find already a considerable number of seafaring men at the towns of Port Royal and Kingston that can't find employment, who I am very apprehensive, for want of occupation in their way, may in a short time desert us and turn pirates. [2]

The governor was right to worry. In the ten years following the treaty, there were probably more pirates in the Caribbean than at any time before or since. Piracy was also widespread along the eastern coast of North America.

Just as Tortuga and Port Royal had been the headquarters for the buccaneers and Madagascar for the Red Sea men, Nassau became the largest base for this final group of pirates. Some two thousand lived in that city by 1717. Nassau was located on New Providence, the chief island in the Bahamas group, which lies southeast of Florida. Like Tortuga and Port Royal, it was ideally placed to give pirates access to valuable shipping.

Good Times and Places for Pirates

Geography and history combined to make the pirates' golden age possible. First, they gave pirates plenty of seagoing merchandise that was worth stealing. In the Caribbean during the 1600s, Spanish ships carried gold, silver, jewels, and other valuable cargo from colonies in Central and South America to the mother country. Thomas Vaughan, the governor of Jamaica during part of the 1670s, noted, "These Indies [the West Indies, another name for the Caribbean area] are so vast and rich, and this kind of rapine [raiding] so sweet, that it is one of the hardest things in the world to draw those from it which have used it for so long." [3] In the 1690s, ships left West Africa with cargoes of freshly captured slaves. On the opposite side of the continent, other ships sailed from India filled with spices, silks, gems, and other goods to be traded in the Middle East for coffee and gold from Africa. By the early 1700s, colonies in North America also provided valuable merchandise.

These same areas provided pirates with good land bases, or havens. An ideal haven lay close to a spot where ships on a common trade route had to sail through a narrow passage, so that pirates could swarm out from the haven and ambush them. The haven had shallow inlets where pirate ships could lurk until their prey sailed by or could hide until searching warships passed. It had protected coves where the pirates could pull their ships up onto the beach to careen them, or scrape off the collection of barnacles and other sea life that attached itself to ships' bottoms and slowed them down. It also offered sources of wood, fresh water, and meat. Some havens included cities where pirates could sell their captured booty and spend the money they received for it. Tortuga, Port Royal, and Nassau were the best havens in the Caribbean. Small islands near Madagascar, such as St. Mary's and Johanna, served the same function in the Indian Ocean.

Help from Governments

The time and places of the golden age also gave pirates a third thing they needed: governments either unwilling or unable to stop them. During most of the golden age, many colonial governments in the Caribbean, Africa, and North America had good reasons to encourage pirates. Some of the colonies counted on the sea rovers for defense. Governor Thomas Modyford of Jamaica, for instance, depended on Henry Morgan's buccaneers to keep the Spanish from attacking that British-held island.

Trade with pirates also brought colonies valuable goods and revenue. A British customs agent in Pennsylvania complained,

> All the persons I have employed in searching for and apprehending these pirates, are abused and affronted [insulted], and called enemies of the country, for disturbing and hindering honest men, as they were pleased to call the pirates, from bringing their money and settling among them.[4]

Finally, piracy helped colonies work around restrictive laws such as the Navigation Acts, which forbade British colonies to trade with any country except England and enforced prices and taxes that benefited Britain but harmed the colonies.

Even when colonies wanted to stop pirates from cruising in their waters, they usually could not do so. Their European mother countries had laws against piracy, but those countries did little to enforce

Two pirates beach their boat in a hidden inlet in order to monitor trade ships.

the laws during the golden age. They had relatively small navies and were at war with one another for much of this period, so they could not spare many warships to patrol distant colonial waters. In 1715, for instance, the British navy assigned only four large and two small warships to the entire Caribbean. Navy ships could almost always defeat a pirate ship if they caught one, but they seldom did.

Attractions of Pirate Life

Throughout the golden age, plenty of people were eager to become pirates. Most were men in their twenties who had had previous sailing experience. Some became sea rovers after they lost their jobs as sailors on merchant, navy, or privateer ships. Others revolted, or mutinied, against cruel captains, seized control of their ships, and began pirate expeditions on their own. Still others joined pirate crews after the pirates captured the ships they had been sailing on. Pirates sometimes forced captured crew members to join them, especially if the men were "sea artists," or sailors with special skills, such as surgeons (essential to the health of a crew) or carpenters (essential to the health of a ship). Often, though, sailors on captured ships joined pirate crews willingly. For a number of reasons, they expected life on a pirate ship to be better than life on a navy or merchant vessel.

Fancifully depicted, captain William Kidd (center) and his crew entertain ladies onboard their pirate ship, where leisure was commonplace.

First, a pirate's life seemed romantic and exciting to people at the time, just as it did to those who read about it later. Even some of the pirates themselves apparently saw it that way. Pirate leader Bartholomew Roberts is quoted as saying,

> In an honest service [legal sailing], there is thin commons [little food], low wages, and hard labor; in this [pirate life], plenty and society, pleasure and ease, liberty and power; and who would not balance creditor on this side [say that pirate life is more desirable] when all the hazard [risk] that is run for it, at worst, is only a sour look or two at choking [a small risk of being hanged]?[5]

Sailors knew that work on a pirate ship was likely to be easier than work on other ships because pirate ships usually carried larger crews for their size. A one hundred–ton merchant ship typically had a crew of only twelve men, for instance, but a pirate ship of the same size might well carry eighty. This difference existed because merchant captains wanted to use as little space and supplies for sailors as possible, whereas pirate captains wanted large numbers of crewmen on hand to attack other ships. In between battles, the pirate ship's large crew meant that the work of sailing the ship was divided among more people, so each sailor had less to do.

The hope of gaining a share of the proceeds from capturing a ship with an extremely valuable cargo—in other words, "treasure"—also lured many sailors into pirating. To be sure, this happened far less often than most of them liked to think. According to David Cordingly, former curator of the National Maritime Museum in Greenwich, England, and an expert on pirates, a typical haul from a seized vessel was "a few bales of silk and cotton, some barrels of tobacco, an anchor cable, some spare sails, the carpenter's tools, and half a dozen black slaves."[6] Still, like winning the lottery today, seizing a ship full of treasure was something to dream about.

The Promise of Freedom

Perhaps the most compelling reason for wanting to be a pirate, though, was the promise of freedom. On navy and merchant ships, the captain was king. He could order sailors to be beaten almost to death or work them to exhaustion, and they usually could do nothing about it. The British writer Samuel Johnson commented satirically that, "no man will be a sailor who [can] . . . get himself into a jail; for being in a ship is being in jail with the chance of being drowned. . . . A man in jail has more room, better food, and commonly better company."[7]

Although pirate ships offered the promise of freedom, they also administered strict punishment. On this ship individuals are made to walk the plank for violating the ships rules.

Pirate ships, on the other hand, were rough-and-ready democracies. Each sailor who joined a pirate crew signed a list of articles, or rules, that governed everyone on the ship. These articles described how plunder was to be divided, how the crew was expected to behave, and what punishments could be given for breaking the rules. The crew voted to choose both the destination of each voyage and the captain. The captain received little more loot than other crew members. He could demand unquestioning obedience only during battle or while chasing a prize ship.

The opportunity for equal treatment aboard a pirate ship must have been especially appealing to men of African descent—and there were many of these among pirate crews. Bartholomew Roberts, for instance, had a crew of 180 white and 48 black sailors in 1721. Slaves carried aboard ships that pirates took over were usually sold just like other captured merchandise, but black sailors on a prize ship's crew might be offered a chance to join the pirates. Runaway slaves or unemployed freedmen also sometimes joined the crews. They were likely to be given the hardest work aboard the ship, but if they were good sailors, they had a better chance of fair treatment than they would have had in most other places. The same applied to the few brave women who managed to join pirate crews, such as Anne Bonny and Mary Read.

To be sure, pirate crews had some problems that merchant and navy crews did not share. Most obviously, they could be sentenced to death if they were caught—but most pirates considered this a small risk. Like privateers, they received no wages other than their shares of the cargoes they seized; the rule was "no prey, no pay." Furthermore, because their activities were illegal, pirates risked being arrested if they came into most harbors to careen their ships or buy food and other supplies. They had to obtain supplies from havens or from the ships they captured.

Pirate Ships

Pirates usually took not only their ships' supplies but also the ships themselves from among the vessels they seized. Their favorite was a type of ship called a sloop, which had a single mast and two large sails. A sloop's relatively small size and narrow shape helped it move quickly and change direction easily. These features were useful when chasing down a prize or running from a warship. Its shallow hull made it able to navigate inlets or lagoons where larger ships would smash onto rocks or become stuck in the sand. A sloop was also a very seaworthy ship, able to survive long voyages and fierce storms.

In reoutfitting a captured ship for his own use, a pirate captain usually added guns to make the ship more heavily armed. (Even merchant ships of the time carried guns, but they did not have many.) Using the guns extensively, however, was a last resort. The pirates' aim, after all, was not to destroy the ships they chased but to seize control of them. They tried to do so with as little risk as possible to their own lives and to the ships' valuable cargoes.

Surprise and Terror

The pirates' chief weapons in capturing ships were not guns but surprise and terror. Surprise came first. If a ship sailed near an island

Pirates often rely on surprise and terror to capture much larger merchant vessels.

where pirates had a base, the pirates might creep up on it in canoes or small open boats. At sea, they might hoist a flag that showed the same nationality that they guessed a merchant ship had, to fool the other ship's crew into thinking that they were friends.

When the pirates were close enough to hail the merchant ship and demand its surrender, terror took over. One element of terror was the pirate flag, which they often hoisted at this time. This flag was sometimes called the Jolly Roger, but no one is sure where the name came from. Because some pirate flags were bloodred, it may have come from the French phrase *jolie rouge*, or "pretty red." Another possibility is that it came from "old Roger," an English nickname for the devil.

Most people think that all pirate flags were black and showed a white skull above crossed bones. In fact, however, each pirate captain had his own flag design. Blackbeard's flag, for instance, showed a skeleton holding an hourglass and stabbing a heart that dripped bright red blood onto a black background.

The purpose of the pirate flag was to frighten the captain and crew of a merchant ship into surrendering without a fight. For the same reason, the pirates sometimes began their attack by firing their guns in front of the ship to show their strength. If the merchant captain surrendered (which he signaled by lowering his ship's flag), he was often told to send boats to the pirate ship to pick up a crew who would take over his vessel. The captain himself might have to go aboard the pirate ship as a hostage.

A Pirate Attack

If a merchant captain refused to surrender, the pirates tried to sail close enough to throw grappling hooks over the side of his ship and pull it against the pirate ship. The pirates then leaped across to the merchant ship's deck, often making a fearsome racket by shouting, striking metal objects, beating on drums, and blowing on horns. They were likely to win a hand-to-hand fight, since they usually outnumbered the merchant crew and were also better armed. Pirates often carried several pistols strapped to their bodies—a necessity because guns of the time could not be reloaded quickly—as well as cutlasses or other large knives.

If captains and crews surrendered and gave up their valuables without a fight, pirates usually (though by no means always) spared their lives. Officers and crew members who decided not to join the pirates might be sent ashore in a small boat at the next port the ship came to. On the other hand, crews and especially captains who opposed the pirates might well be tortured. So might wealthy-looking passengers aboard ships or residents of towns raided by pirates like Henry Morgan. Some pirate leaders seemed to enjoy torture for its own sake, but most saw it simply as the fastest way to get what they wanted. Their behavior was cruel, but it was by no means uncommon in their time. Governments routinely used torture to make prisoners confess, for instance.

Once a captured ship's cargo was divided and sold, pirate crews usually went ashore at some welcoming port and spent all their money on a mammoth party. Only a few, like Henry Morgan, were smart enough to invest their earnings in something that would last, like land. Even fewer buried their treasure, as pirates in books and movies are so fond of doing. Gold and jewels did them no good under the ground.

End of the Golden Age

Changes in trade, combined with the pirates' own success, eventually brought their golden age to an end. By the 1720s, colonies in the Americas had become stronger and more prosperous. They no longer needed pirates to defend them or to supply them with trade goods. On the contrary, as the colonies' legal trade increased, their governments came to see the pirates as a major threat to their economic health. For instance, around 1718 the governor and council of the colony of South Carolina wrote to Britain that unless an additional warship was sent to protect them from pirates, "our trade must be inevitably ruined." [8]

With more and more colonial governments and European-owned merchant companies complaining about the pirates, Britain and other European countries finally began to listen. They sent more warships to the Caribbean, North America, and Africa to hunt pirates or guard valuable merchant fleets. They offered pardons to pirates who reformed and rewards to people who captured pirates. When they caught pirate crews, they tried and hanged them quickly and in large numbers. As a result of these measures, the number of pirates dropped rapidly in the early 1720s. About two thousand pirates were active in the seas off the Americas in 1720, but by 1723 that number had been cut in half, and by 1726 it was down to a mere two hundred.

In the 1720s British navy warships policed the trade routes between the Americas, ending the golden age of piracy.

Books About Buccaneers

While authorities were cracking down on pirates, the public in Europe and America grew fascinated by them—horrified and yet attracted, as some people are by mass murderers today. Popular ballads and newspaper accounts described pirates' wicked deeds. Several authors also wrote best-selling books about pirates. These books are some of the chief sources of information about famous pirates' lives.

Two books, in particular, shaped people's views of pirates from their own time to the present. The first was written by a Frenchman named Alexander Exquemelin, who sailed with Henry Morgan and his buccaneers as a surgeon. Exquemelin's book described the daily life of the early buccaneers and Morgan's attacks on Spanish cities in Central America. It was first published in Dutch in 1678 and appeared in English as *The Buccaneers of America* in 1684.

The second famous pirate book, *A General History of the Robberies and Murders of the Most Notorious Pirates,* was published in Britain in 1724, just a few years after public execution of pirates was at its height. It contained biographies of the most famous British pirates, from Blackbeard to Bartholomew Roberts. "Captain Charles Johnson" was given as the *General History's* author, but no independent record of Johnson's existence has been found. Some modern scholars believe that the book was written by Daniel Defoe, a well-known British author who wrote both factual newspaper stories and novels such as *Robinson Crusoe.* Other historians say there is no good evidence that Defoe wrote the book. The identity of the *General History's* author may always remain a mystery.

Many of the facts in Johnson's and Exquemelin's books can be confirmed in other sources, such as records of pirates' trials. Unfortunately for people who want to know the truth about pirates, however, both authors saw nothing wrong with exaggerating some features of the events they wrote about or even mixing fact and fiction. For instance, historians think they sometimes exaggerated pirates' cruelties to please the bloodthirsty public of the time. Johnson invented conversations and sometimes whole histories.

More Accurate Information

Other sources provide more accurate information about the pirates of the golden age. Government records of pirates' trials often included lengthy statements from both the pirates and their victims. Some ship captains—including a few pirates and privateers, such as William Dampier and Woodes Rogers—kept diaries or logbooks in which they described captures of ships and travels to exotic lands.

Archaeologists have also found the remains of several vessels known or suspected to be pirate ships. The first to be discovered was the *Whydah*, a converted slave ship used by a pirate named Sam Bellamy. It was found off Cape Cod in 1984. More recently, ships thought to belong to William Kidd, Blackbeard, Henry Morgan, and William Dampier have been uncovered. Objects taken from these ships should provide fascinating insights into the way pirates lived and worked.

The Pirates' Effects on History

The truth about pirates has proved to be as exciting as any fiction— and the truth is that these sea rovers had important effects on history. They helped to break Spain's stranglehold on the Americas, allowing British, French, and Dutch colonies to establish them-

An archaeologist examines a recovered part of the pirate ship Whydah.

selves there. They brought valuable trade to these struggling colonies. Later, on the other hand, they damaged trade. The need to control the pirates forced Britain and other European countries to expand their navies and recognize the importance of long-distance trade. It also led to agreements between countries that helped to lay the foundation for international law.

Ironically, in the course of rebelling against authority, the pirates of the golden age helped to create a world in which authority was strong enough to make their continued existence impossible. At the same time, however, they created a dream of freedom and adventure that will never die.

CHAPTER 2

Henry Morgan: The Clever Pirate

Although Henry Morgan is the best known and most successful of the buccaneers of the first part of the pirates' golden age, he fought most of his battles on land rather than at sea. In those battles he showed himself a master of strategy, defeating Spanish forts and cities by clever plans and tricks more than by force. He was also a talented leader, able to hold the loyalty of hundreds of quarrelsome buccaneers and also to gain friends in the highest ranks of both colonial and English society. Unlike most of his buccaneering companions, he died a wealthy man.

Conflicting Stories

Morgan never spoke or wrote about his childhood, so almost nothing is known of it. In a document he signed in 1665 he stated that he was thirty years old, so he was probably born in 1635. He was born in Wales, on the western side of Britain, most likely in either Llanrhymni or Pencarn. Alexander Exquemelin, who took part in several of Morgan's raids and wrote extensively about them, said that Morgan's father was "a well-to-do farmer." [9] However, a "corrected" version of Exquemelin's book, issued after Morgan threatened to sue its publisher for libel, stated that Morgan was "a gentleman's son." [10] This is possible, because Morgan is known to have had two uncles, Colonel Sir Edward Morgan and Major General Sir Thomas Morgan, who were high-ranking British military leaders.

"Having no liking for farm work," Exquemelin wrote, Morgan "decided to go to sea." [11] Exquemelin stated that after Morgan arrived in the Caribbean, he worked as a servant on the island of Barbados. This claim seems to have angered Morgan more than anything else in Exquemelin's book. Morgan insisted that he "never was a servant to anybody in his life." [12] Instead, he said, he had come to the West Indies as a soldier.

Morgan was not the only member of his family to reach Jamaica. His uncle Sir Edward Morgan was Jamaica's deputy governor from

1664 until his death in 1665. Soon after Edward Morgan died, Henry married the older man's daughter (and his own first cousin), Mary Elizabeth. All that is known of their married life is that twenty-three years later, Morgan's will called Mary Elizabeth "his very well and entirely beloved wife" [13] and left the bulk of his estate to her.

Buccaneer Admiral

By 1665, Henry Morgan was an experienced fighter on sea and land. He was vice admiral, or second in command, to Edward Mansfield, then head of the Jamaica buccaneers. When Mansfield died suddenly the following year, the buccaneers chose Morgan to be their new leader.

The new "admiral" of the buccaneers worked closely with Jamaica's governor, Sir Thomas Modyford. Each man had much to offer the other. Spain claimed the right to control all land in the Caribbean, and Modyford and other Jamaican leaders feared that Spanish forces might try to recapture their island at any time. Modyford felt that the buccaneers, most of whom were seasoned fighters, were Jamaica's only defense. He also valued the wealth that they brought to island cities such as Port Royal. Morgan, in turn, valued Modyford's power to make his activities legal. Morgan always claimed that he was a privateer rather than a pirate because he carried letters of marque from Modyford that authorized him to attack the Spanish.

For his strategy and shrewdness, Henry Morgan is considered the most successful buccaneer.

The Siege of Porto Bello

Morgan's first major venture as leader of the Jamaican buccaneers was an attack on the Spanish city of Porto Bello, on the Caribbean side of the Isthmus of Panama. Mule trains carried silver from mines in Peru to this "beautiful port" to be loaded onto treasure galleons heading for Spain. Three forts bristling with cannons and soldiers guarded Porto Bello from attacks by sea, but Morgan learned that the city was weakly defended on its landward side. No one expected raiders to hack their way through the swamps and rain forest that surrounded its rear. Therefore, Morgan decided, that was just what his buccaneers would do.

Staying well out of sight of Porto Bello's harbor, the buccaneers quietly landed their fleet of nine ships and about 460 men at the mouth of a river thirty miles west of the town in July 1668. At nightfall they lowered twenty-three large canoes from the ships, and most of the buccaneers climbed into them. They rowed along the shore until they came to a spot near the port, hid the boats in the forest, and crept through the jungle toward the city.

The buccaneers took the first fort by surprise. The second one fought harder. After trying unsuccessfully all morning to capture it, Morgan developed a desperate, ruthless plan. He and his men built a dozen sturdy wooden ladders, tall enough to reach the top of the fort's walls. He then rounded up all the monks and nuns among the pirates' prisoners and forced them to carry the ladders to the fort. Morgan hoped that the Spaniards' well-known respect for religious people would make the soldiers hold their fire. This did not happen, however, and many of the unfortunate ladder bearers lost their lives. Once the ladders were in place, the buccaneers scrambled up them and soon took over the fort. Those in the third fort, having seen the other two fall, quickly surrendered.

Surrounded by Morgan's buccaneers, the Spanish governor dies defending Porto Bello in 1668.

A Rich Haul

The sounds of fighting had alerted Porto Bello's citizens. Some, still in their nightclothes, swarmed into the streets when the attacks began, running for shelter inside the forts. Others dumped their treasures down wells in the hope that the buccaneers would not find them, then fled into the forest. Once Morgan's men controlled the town, they began searching it for hidden treasure and combing the forest to round up the people who had hidden there.

Exquemelin, who was with the buccaneers at Porto Bello, says that they systematically tortured many of the people they captured until they revealed where their gold and jewels were hidden—or until they died. He may have exaggerated these stories somewhat, but other reports confirm that Morgan's men used torture during their raids. Terrible as this was, it was not unusual for the time.

During the month they spent in Porto Bello, the buccaneers extracted considerable wealth from its citizens. They also gained a ransom for the town itself by threatening to burn it if the money was not paid. Their total takings came to about 215,000 pieces of eight (a common Spanish silver coin) plus silks, silver, jewels, and three hundred slaves. Each man received enough money to pay for a tremendous party when the group returned to Jamaica in triumph around August 17. Pirate historian David Cordingly calls the capture of Porto Bello "one of the most successful amphibious [land and water] operations of the seventeenth century."[14]

Bottled Up in a Lake

In March 1669, Morgan and about five hundred men raided Maracaibo and Gibraltar, two towns at opposite ends of Lake Maracaibo in Venezuela. Capturing the towns proved easier than leaving them. The buccaneers returned to Maracaibo from Gibraltar, on the inland side of the lake, to find three heavily armed Spanish warships waiting for them near the narrow passage that separated the lake from the sea, trapping their ships inside the lake. A fort on an island near the lake mouth had also been restocked with guns and soldiers. The leader of the Spanish forces gave Morgan two days to agree to sail away and leave all his plunder behind or else be attacked by the troops.

Once again Morgan used cleverness to accomplish what strength could not. During the two days of grace, he had his men fill a small ship with gunpowder, tar, and all the other flammable material they could find. They then painted logs black to make them look like cannons and jammed them into the ship's gun ports. They assembled scarecrowlike wooden figures, dressed them in sailors' clothes and caps, and propped them against the deck rails to make the ship appear to be carrying a large crew. In reality, only about a dozen buccaneers stayed aboard the ship—just enough to keep it moving.

At dawn on May 1, these brave men sailed the disguised ship up to the largest Spanish warship, the *Magdalena*. They pulled the two ships together with grappling hooks as if they intended to board the warship for a hand-to-hand fight. They then lit the material on the fire ship, jumped overboard, and swam for their lives. A moment later the ship exploded into a ball of flame, blowing a hole in the side of the *Magdalena* and sinking it. The second Spanish warship beat such a hasty retreat that it ran into the shore of the fort's island and also sank. The buccaneers easily captured the third one. A day or two later they even sent divers down to the remains of the *Magdalena*, bringing up fifteen thousand pieces of eight and an assortment of silver and jewels.

A Clever Trick

Morgan's men were not home free, however. Spanish soldiers still held the island fort that guarded their passage to the open sea. Once again Morgan's strategy came to the rescue. Taking an approach opposite to the one he had used in Porto Bello, he made a great show of lowering canoes filled with armed men from his ships and sending them around the rear of the island. Two or three men then rowed each boat back to the ships, where they appeared to pick up another load of buccaneers.

Seeing the boats repeat this round-trip many times, the Spanish soldiers concluded that a huge force of buccaneers was being brought to the island to attack the fort by land. They therefore turned their cannons to face the landward side of the island. That night, Morgan had his ships drift stealthily toward the now-unguarded mouth of the strait. They then hoisted their sails and made a quick getaway with all their loot and crews. He had fooled the Spanish by having a single batch of crewmen make the trip in the boats over and over again, lying down during each return journey to make the boats appear empty.

A New Call to War

When Morgan and his fleet returned to Jamaica on May 17, they learned from Governor Modyford that they needed to be quiet for a while. Britain was trying to make peace with Spain, and British officials had ordered Modyford to make the buccaneers stay home. They therefore settled down to drink up or otherwise spend their profits. Morgan, more sensibly, used his share to buy a house and a sugar plantation. He later bought other plantations as well.

Spain soon gave the buccaneers the excuse they needed to go to sea once more. The crew of a Spanish warship burned a few houses on Jamaica in June 1670. Modyford and the island's governing council therefore declared a state of emergency and made Henry Morgan commander of all Jamaican warships. They urged him to make another raid to distract the Spanish from attacking Jamaica.

Morgan used men in canoes to trick the Spanish into believeing a huge force of men was preparing to attack Maracaibo.

In October 1670, Morgan gathered men and ships from all over the Caribbean. "The success of his former voyages . . . made him popular even with those who had never set eyes on him,"[15] Exquemelin wrote. Morgan eventually commanded thirty-six ships and about 1,850 men—an impressive navy, even though most of the ships were small.

A Painful Journey

Morgan and his captains decided to attack the city of Panama, on the Pacific side of the isthmus then called Darien. Panama was the capital of Darien and the richest city in Spanish America. Gold and silver from Peru were brought here before being sent across the isthmus to Porto Bello.

Morgan planned to approach Panama overland, following the Chagre River. He sent one of his captains to take over the fort that guarded the river mouth. After the fort had been secured, he put about twelve hundred of his men into canoes and flat-bottomed riverboats and started up the Chagre on January 18, 1671. He thought the group would need less than a week to reach Panama, a mere forty-eight miles away. He decided not to weigh the men down with food supplies, believing that they could steal food from farms or homesteads along the way.

For once, Morgan made a bad choice. A deserter had warned Panama that he was coming, and the Spanish had destroyed everything edible in the area. By the fourth day of their march, the buccaneers were so hungry that when they found a heap of leather bags, they roasted the bags and ate them "with as much gusto [appetite] as if leather were meat—and so it was, in their imagination," Exquemelin wrote. "They even fought over it." [16] Only the lucky discovery of a barn full of maize (corn) that had somehow escaped destruction kept them from starving. Their journey through mosquito-infested swamps and steaming jungles took nine exhausting days.

Morgan Takes Panama

The buccaneers finally met Spanish troops on an open plain near Panama on January 28. The Spanish had twice as many men as Morgan, but most were untrained and poorly armed. They had intended to drive a large herd of cattle into the buccaneer ranks to panic the invaders, but this plan failed when the cattle panicked instead and ran away. Most of the Spanish soldiers soon followed.

Soon after the buccaneers entered Panama, the city caught fire. The fire may have started by accident, or fleeing Spanish soldiers may have set the town ablaze rather than let the buccaneers have it. Before long, most of the city was wiped out. "Thus was consumed that famous and ancient city of Panama, which is the greatest mart [market] for silver and gold in the whole world," [17] Morgan later wrote in his report to Governor Modyford.

As soon as the flames died down, the raiders began sifting through the ruins and searching the surrounding forest for potential prisoners. They brought back many townspeople and forced them to reveal the location of their hidden possessions or send messages to relatives asking for ransom. They were frustrated to learn, however, that while they had been slogging through the jungle, ships had sailed away bearing most of the gold and silver that had been stored in the town.

Even so, the buccaneers' take from Panama was even greater than that from Porto Bello: about 750,000 pieces of eight as well as gold

Morgan's well-trained and experienced buccaneers easily sack Panama.

and silver bars, jewels, spices, and silks. On February 24, after about three weeks in the city, Morgan brought the buccaneers' loot back across the isthmus on mules, then divided it before the men boarded their ships. The amount that each crew member received apparently was less than the men had expected, so a number of the buccaneers, including Exquemelin, concluded that Morgan was cheating them. Whether this was true or not, Morgan decided that he should leave the group quickly. He and a few of his captains sailed for Jamaica on March 6, leaving the rest of the band to make their way home however they could.

Sent to England

The governor and council greeted Morgan with a vote of thanks. They soon learned, however, that the government in England did not share their enthusiasm. Britain had signed a peace treaty with Spain in 1670, so Morgan's raid on Panama had been illegal, and Spanish officials had become very upset when they found out about it. Wanting to calm the Spanish and keep the new peace, Britain's King Charles II ordered Governor Modyford brought to England to be put on trial. A ship took him out of Jamaica in August 1671. The following spring, Morgan, too, was taken to England "to answer for his offences against the King, his crown and dignity." [18]

The king did not follow through on these harsh orders, however. He imprisoned Modyford in the Tower of London for two years, but Modyford had every comfort during his stay and was never put on trial. Morgan was not even imprisoned. On the contrary, he met the cream of British nobility, and his power to charm and impress people proved to work just as well on them as it had on the rough buccaneers. His new friends spoke in his favor when the Board of Trade considered his misdeeds, and he was not punished.

While Morgan (seated on a barrel) interrogated the townspeople of Panama about their hidden possessions, Spanish ships escaped with the treasure.

Indeed, in January 1674, less than two years after Morgan had arrived in England in disgrace, King Charles made him deputy governor of Jamaica, the second-highest post on the island, and lieutenant general of the Jamaican armed forces. Praising Morgan's "loyalty, prudence and courage, and long experience in that colony," [19] the king even gave the old buccaneer a knighthood, making him Sir Henry Morgan. Modyford, too, was released from the Tower and returned to Jamaica as chief justice.

Changing Political Winds

Morgan sailed in and out of political favor several times during the next few years. When Spain threatened new aggression against Jamaica, the king asked Morgan's advice about the best ways to defend the island. Morgan had a chance to strengthen its defenses

King Charles II (pictured here) appointed Morgan the deputy governor of Jamaica.

himself during several brief periods as acting governor. On the other hand, some of Jamaica's new governors disliked and distrusted him. One, Lord Vaughan, accused him of "drinking and gaming [gambling] at the taverns" [20] and making secret deals with his old buccaneer friends.

In reality, however, whatever his personal feelings might have been, Morgan sensed that public opinion in Jamaica had turned against the buccaneers. Jamaicans now usually felt secure from Spanish attack, and the island's rich planters wanted to encourage peaceful trade. Applying his cleverness as effectively to his political career as he had to his attacks against the Spanish, Morgan therefore announced that he was now an enemy of privateers and pirates alike. He encouraged the buccaneers to accept government pardons and settle down and, as judge of the island's Vice Admiralty Court, promised to execute them if they did not. "I have put to death, imprisoned and transported to the Spaniard for execution all English and Spanish pirates that I could get within this government," [21] he told British officials.

Last Days

Not everyone believed the old buccaneer. After finding himself on the losing side of some political quarrels, he lost his government posts in the early 1680s. By that time, too, his health was failing. A visiting doctor described him as "lean, sallow-coloured [with yellowish skin], his eyes a little yellowish, and belly a little jutting out or prominent"[22]—all signs of the liver damage that alcoholism had produced.

Henry Morgan died on August 25, 1688. In honor of the important positions he had held in Jamaica's government, he was given a state funeral. All the ships in the harbor fired their guns to salute him.

Four years later, Port Royal, the city that had been Morgan's buccaneer haven, died as well. A tremendous earthquake struck the town on the sand spit on June 7, 1692, followed by a tidal wave powerful enough to push a ship up onto one of its main streets. By the time the quake was over, most of what some people had called the wickedest city in the world had sunk beneath the sea. Nature itself seemed to be underlining the fact that the first part of the pirates' golden age, the era of the buccaneers, was over.

CHAPTER 3

William Dampier: The Explorer Pirate

Even as a child, William Dampier studied the world around him intensely. Born on a small farm in East Coker, Somerset, in the west of England, in August 1651, Dampier wrote later that he had studied the qualities of the different fields that people farmed in the area:

> I [be]came acquainted with them all, and knew what each would produce, viz. [that is], wheat, barley, beans, peas, oats, flax or hemp; in all which I had more than usual knowledge for one so young, taking a particular delight in observing it. [23]

William Dampier contributed greatly to scientists' knowledge of meteorology and geography.

Dampier showed that same delight in observation when, as a member of several buccaneering crews, he sailed around the world three times and kept careful notes of everything he saw. The books he made from his diaries not only provided vivid pictures of a pirate's daily life but also added greatly to scientists' knowledge of winds, ocean currents, geography, and the plants, animals, and native peoples of exotic lands.

Young Man in Jamaica

After receiving a basic education in his village, Dampier, "complying with the inclination I had very early of seeing the world,"[24] became an apprentice to an experienced seaman, assisting him and in return being taught his trade. He gained sailing experience in two long-distance voyages and a brief term in the Royal Navy. He left the navy because of illness and returned to Somerset.

Colonel William Helyar, the chief landowner in the area, offered Dampier a chance to work on a plantation in Jamaica that Helyar owned. The young man eagerly accepted, but when he reached the island in 1674, he was disappointed. He had thought he was going to help manage the plantation, but the man in charge there treated him like a servant. Dampier quit the job a few months later.

A Brutal Existence

After about a year, Dampier left Jamaica and joined men who were cutting down a type of tree called logwood near Campeche Bay, on the coast of Honduras in Central America. A valuable red dye was made from the wood of this tree. Harvesting it was brutal work, done in steaming swamps infested with mosquitoes and alligators. The logwood cutters, many of whom were part-time buccaneers, gave Dampier his first taste of life among pirates.

Dampier was already keeping a diary of his experiences by this time. For example, he wrote this description of monkeys that lived in the area:

> The monkeys that are in these parts are the ugliest I ever saw. They are much bigger than a hare [rabbit], and have great tails about two foot and a half long. . . . The first time I met them they were a great company, dancing from tree to tree, over my head; chattering and making a terrible noise; and a great many grim faces, and showing antic [crazy-looking] gestures. . . . [One] monkey caught hold of [a] bough with the tip of his tail, and there continued swinging to and fro and making mouths at me.[25]

Dampier returned briefly to England in August 1678 and married a woman named Judith. She apparently was a maid in the Duchess of Grafton's household, but nothing else is known about her. She probably saw little—perhaps nothing—of her wandering husband after their wedding.

Buccaneering Voyages

Dampier went back to the West Indies in 1679. "More to indulge my curiosity than to get wealth,"[26] he later claimed, he joined a buccaneering band. During the next several years he saw battles, mutinies, several changes of ships and captains, and a good deal of Central and South America. In 1683, as a crewman on another buccaneering voy-

Caught in a typhoon in 1688, Dampier's ship sails off course, sending him toward the coast of Australia.

age, he sailed around South America to attack Spanish settlements on the Pacific side of the continent. He joined a third group of buccaneers in 1686 and traveled to the Far East. Dampier was happy to keep on the move, "knowing that the farther we went, the more knowledge and experience I should get, which was the main thing I regarded." [27]

At the beginning of 1688, as Dampier's ship was sailing westward from Asia, a fierce tropical storm called a typhoon drove it off course. "By 12 o'clock at night it blew exceeding hard and the rain poured down as through a sieve," he wrote later. "It thundered and lightened prodigiously, and the sea seemed all of a fire about us; for every sea that broke sparkled like lightning." [28] On January 4 the crew sighted the barren northwestern coast of Australia. At the time, this land was known as New Holland because the only European explorers who had visited it until then had been Dutch. Dampier and the other crew members, in fact, were the first English people to land on the continent. They went ashore and careened their ship, remaining there two months.

After many more adventures, Dampier finally worked his way back to England on September 16, 1691. He was now forty years old and had been away for more than twelve years. His buccaneering journeys had taken him around the world.

Dampier's Treasure

Dampier's travels had netted him very little money, yet he did bring home treasure. From the beginning of his days in the West Indies, he had kept a diary in which he described not only the events of his life as a pirate but also the plants, animals, and human natives of each place he visited. He hung on to this journal through sea battles, hurricanes, and shipwrecks. "I took care to provide myself with a large joint of bamboo, which I stopped at both ends, closing it with wax, so as to keep out any water," he wrote later. "In this I preserved my journal and other writings from being wet, though I was often forced to swim." [29]

After returning to England, Dampier turned his diary into a book. Called *A New Voyage Round the World*, it was published in 1697 and immediately became a best-seller. With its fascinating details of far-off places, it appealed to the growing number of people who enjoyed reading about others' travels. The many readers of Alexander Exquemelin's tales of Henry Morgan were also happy to see another true adventure story about pirates.

Dampier's publishers soon asked him to add a second volume. It included descriptions of his life as a logwood cutter, a visit to what is now Vietnam, and an essay on winds, tides, and ocean currents in the tropics. This book appeared in 1699 and also sold well. In a biography of Dampier, Christopher Lloyd writes, "His wind map of the Pacific is the first of its kind. It was an amazingly comprehensive compilation by one man." [30]

In addition to being enjoyable travel literature, Dampier's books were valuable scientific documents. The techniques and philosophy of science were just starting to be developed at this time. The scientists of the day, pioneers such as Sir Isaac Newton, stressed the importance of carefully observing the natural world, which is exactly what Dampier did. Other Europeans had visited the places he described, but few, if any, had written about them in such detail. About 135 years later, the same kinds of observations, made in many of the same places, would lead Charles Darwin to develop the theory of evolution.

Voyage to New Holland

Dampier's books sent him to sea again, under circumstances very different from those of his previous voyages. The president of the Royal Society, Britain's chief scientific organization, admired Dampier's writing and introduced him to the head of the British navy. Learning that the navy wanted to find out more about New Holland, Dampier proposed that the government give him funding for a voyage of ex-

38

ploration there. The secretary of the Admiralty agreed in November 1698. According to Simon Craig, writing in the March 1998 issue of *Geographical Magazine,* this "seems to have been the first voyage of straightforward exploration ever commissioned by the British government."[31]

The Admiralty's support was not overly generous. The *Roebuck,* the warship it gave Dampier, was in poor condition. His crew of fifty was untrained in exploration, and some feared making such a long voyage. Others, including Dampier's second-in-command, Lieutenant George Fisher, disliked serving under an ex-pirate. Some other former pirates who had been given navy ships had gone back to their old way of life, taking the ships with them, and Fisher apparently was afraid that Dampier would do the same.

Dampier departed for Australia in January 1699. He and Fisher clashed from the beginning. Finally, as the *Roebuck* neared the coast of Brazil, Fisher defied one order too many and called Dampier an "old rogue." Dampier lost his temper—always an easy thing for him—and struck Fisher with his cane. He then ordered the lieutenant to be kept in chains in a small, hot cabin. When the *Roebuck* reached Bahia three weeks later, Dampier turned Fisher over to authorities there and had him jailed for three months.

A Difficult Journey

Thinking no more about his rebellious lieutenant, Dampier repaired and resupplied his ship and continued southward some seven thousand miles to New Holland. The *Roebuck* reached its first Australian landfall, an island off Australia's west coast called Dirk Hartog's Island

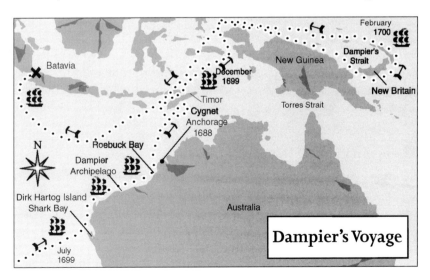

Dampier's Voyage

after an earlier explorer, around the end of July. Dampier named the bay near the island Shark Bay because so many of these fearsome creatures swam there. He then turned north, hoping to find the spot where his ship had landed on his earlier trip because he knew he could get fresh water there.

Continuing to find nothing but barrenness, Dampier's group finally turned the northwestern corner of the continent and began sailing east. He had to abandon his explorations before he reached Australia's east coast, however, because both his crew and his ship had developed serious problems. Unable to find much fresh water or food, the crew was showing signs of scurvy, a severe illness that was then common among sailors on long sea voyages. (It is now known to be caused by a lack of vitamin C, a nutrient found in many fresh fruits and vegetables.) Furthermore, the unfortunate *Roebuck* was starting to leak. At a spot now called Roebuck Bay, Dampier and his men turned away from the Australian coast and headed north to the island of Timor. They refreshed their food and water supplies and cleaned and repaired their ship as best they could, then proceeded northeast to the large island called New Guinea.

As he nears the fiery, volcanic Ascension Island, Dampier realizes the Roebuck *will sink.*

Dampier added considerably to what was known about the coastlines of northern Australia and southern New Guinea and the currents in the stretch of ocean between them. He visited a small island called New Britain and showed that it was separated from the main part of New Guinea by a strait, or narrow stretch of water, now called Dampier Strait. According to Christopher Lloyd, this was the major finding of his voyage. Dampier failed, however, to make the far more important discovery that New Guinea and Australia were separate and that a ship could sail all the way to the continent's fertile east coast. Europeans would not learn that fact until British explorer James Cook made a similar journey some seventy years later.

As the *Roebuck* sailed past New Guinea, its condition grew worse.

Dampier and his men are forced to live on Ascension Island after the Roebuck *begins to sink. Here Dampier speaks with an aborigine while searching for food on the island.*

Dampier tried to patch it up in the Dutch colony of Batavia, now Djakarta in Indonesia, but when the ship neared Ascension Island, a dry, barren volcanic island in the middle of the South Atlantic, he could see that the *Roebuck* was going to sink. On February 24, 1701, he sailed the ship as close to the beach as possible, then he and his crew loaded themselves and what supplies they could save onto a raft and paddled ashore. Dampier had to leave many of his papers behind, although he saved twenty-four plant specimens that he had gathered in western Australia. The men stayed on the island, living on crabs, birds, turtles, and wild goats, until passing ships saw their signals and picked them up four weeks later.

Serious Charges

Dampier returned to London in August 1701. Far from being welcomed as a hero, the battered explorer found himself in serious trouble. While Dampier had been struggling with his leaky ship off Australia, his half-forgotten lieutenant, George Fisher, had returned to England and begun preparing revenge against his former leader. A captain might be free to hit or whip an ordinary seaman, but striking a naval officer was another matter. Fisher brought charges against Dampier before the Lords of the Admiralty, not only for hitting him but also for allegedly making disrespectful statements about the Admiralty's authority, being drunk, and generally mismanaging his command. Other disgruntled crew members supported his complaints.

Fisher's charges led to a court-martial for Dampier on June 8, 1702. The judges found Dampier guilty and fined him all his pay for the Australia voyage. They also ruled that he was "not a fit person to be employed as commander of any of her Majesty's [naval] ships." [32]

Without money once more, Dampier turned again to writing, preparing a book about his trip to New Holland. It contained his usual extensive descriptions of plants, animals, and adventures, which were all the more interesting because Europeans had never seen most of the things he described. *A Voyage to New Holland* was published in 1703, with a second volume added in 1709.

A Failed Privateer

In spite of Dampier's troubles with the *Roebuck,* a group of merchants from London and Bristol soon asked him to lead a privateering expedition in a ship called the *St. George.* A new war between Britain and Spain had broken out in 1702, making privateering against Spain legal once more, and Dampier convinced the merchants that "vast profits and advantages" [33] would result from such a voyage. His good reputation as a navigator apparently outweighed his bad one as a commander in their eyes.

The *St. George,* carrying a crew of 120, and a smaller ship, the *Cinque Ports,* left Ireland in September 1703, bound for South America. It proved to be a miserable journey for all concerned. Again, Dampier disagreed constantly with his officers. "He was . . . so much self-conceited that he would never hear any reason," [34] one wrote later. In addition, he had apparently lost the willingness to fight that he had had in his earlier buccaneering days. He turned away from one potential prize after another, leading many of his men to label him a coward.

The privateers lost nearly every battle they took part in, which the crew blamed largely on Dampier's ineffective leadership. Eventually half of his men deserted him, and the *St. George,* like the *Roebuck,* grew so leaky that it had to be abandoned. Dampier finally returned to England in late 1707, having completed his second trip around the world, but the merchants who had sponsored the journey were so disgusted with him that they sued him for fraud. They later dropped the charges, however.

Master Navigator

In spite of all these disasters, William Dampier and the sea were not through with one another. In 1708, when Dampier was fifty-six years old, a young man named Woodes Rogers, possibly the son of one of Dampier's old shipmates, asked him to be navigator and pilot on an extensive privateering voyage that Rogers was planning. Dampier accepted.

Rogers was as calm as Dampier was hot-tempered. Different as they were, the two apparently respected each other and got along well. Rogers was impressed by Dampier's long experience and great skill as a navigator and mapmaker. Dampier, in turn, was probably glad to leave the challenges of command to Rogers, who had a flair for it that Dampier lacked.

Rogers's two ships, the *Duke* and the *Duchess,* with a combined crew of 330 men, left the British seaport of Bristol on August 2, 1708. Their voyage was far more successful than the one Dampier had led. Its chief prize was one of the Manila galleons, the richly loaded Spanish ships that sailed each year from Asia to Mexico. Rogers's ships returned

Woodes Rogers' crew captures a Manila galleon, due in part to Dampier's immense knowledge of the sea.

to England in October 1711, completing William Dampier's third trip around the world.

Legal wrangles at the end of the voyage kept its considerable profits from being paid out for five years. Dampier did not live long enough to receive his share. However, he was able to borrow enough money from friends to live the remaining three years of his life in relative comfort in London. He died in March 1715.

As commander and pirate, William Dampier left something to be desired. As seaman and navigator, observer and writer, however, his skills were second to none. An article in *Athena Review* called him "one of the most highly regarded map-makers and navigators of all time." [35] Admiral James Burney, who traveled with James Cook and authored an influential nineteenth-century history of discoveries in the South Pacific, wrote of Dampier:

> It is not easy to name another voyager or traveler who has given more useful information to the world; to whom the merchant and mariner [sailor] are so much indebted; or who has communicated his information in a more unembarrassed and intelligible manner. [36]

William Kidd: The Unlucky Pirate

Captain William Kidd became one of the best-known pirates of all time, yet few pirates have deserved their reputation less. Kidd committed several acts of piracy and killed one of his crewmen, but other pirates did far worse and still escaped the hangman's noose. Historians have argued about exactly how much of a villain he was, but they agree on one thing: Kidd was probably the unluckiest pirate who ever lived.

Even less is known about Kidd's early life than about that of most other famous pirates. The only certain fact is that he came from Scotland. Tradition says he was born around 1645 in the port city of Greenock and that his father was a Presbyterian minister.

William Kidd is considered the unluckiest pirate to ever live.

Privateer and Merchant

When Kidd first appeared in historical records in 1689, he was about forty-four years old and had just become the captain of a privateer ship called the *Blessed William*. The commander of an expedition he took part in said that Kidd "fought as well as any man I ever saw,"[37] but Kidd's crew apparently was less pleased with him. Soon afterward they seized control of the *Blessed William* and turned it into a pirate ship.

Pursuing his runaway crew, Kidd went to New York, a British colony where pirates often came to trade. He arrived around the beginning of 1691 and found that he liked the city. He made friends with some of New York's most powerful merchants and married Sarah Bradley Cox Oort, a wealthy widow with two daughters. Before long, Kidd himself was a well-respected merchant.

A New Kind of Expedition

In spite of this comfortable life, Kidd found himself missing the sea. He went to England in 1695, hoping to persuade the British government to make him the captain of either a privateer or a navy ship. There he ran into Robert Livingston, a merchant he had known in New York, and the two developed the idea for an unusual kind of privateering expedition. They knew that the government was very concerned about pirates who were attacking shipping and hurting British trade in the Indian Ocean, yet did not want to spare warships to seek the pirates out. As New York merchants, Kidd and Livingston knew a good deal about these "Red Sea men" because many New Yorkers traded with them regularly. They proposed that instead of attacking the ships of an enemy nation, as privateers usually did, this one would capture pirates—and their valuable booty.

Livingston had recently met Richard Coote, the Earl of Bellomont. He introduced Kidd to the nobleman and told him about their idea. Bellomont was a leading member of the Whigs, the more liberal of the two political parties in Parliament, Britain's legislative body. He had just been made the governor of the Massachusetts Bay Colony and New York.

Bellomont liked the two men's privateering plan. He introduced Livingston and Kidd to other Whig leaders and helped them to persuade several of these politicians to provide most of the money for the expedition in return for a large share of its expected profits. The Whig lords in turn helped Kidd obtain a special privateering license to capture pirates as well as a more usual one entitling him to take ships belonging to citizens of France, with which England was then at war.

Kidd's noble backers provided him with a new three-masted ship, the *Adventure Galley,* that was well suited to be a pirate chaser. It had openings for oars along its sides, so it could be rowed as well as sailed. This meant that it could keep moving even under the windless conditions that sometimes arose in the Red Sea and Indian Ocean. It also could change direction more easily than a ship that depended only on sails.

A Bad-Luck Voyage

Kidd's bad luck began almost as soon as the *Adventure Galley* left London in February 1696. He had handpicked seventy experienced, dependable seamen to serve on his ship's crew, but a navy captain stopped him and seized, or "impressed," about twenty of them for his own crew. Kidd had to stop in New York to collect more crewmen, including some ex-pirates.

The *Adventure Galley* left for Africa on September 6 with a crew of 152. The bad luck continued. Near Madagascar Kidd lost about a third of his men to disease and had to replace them with even more ex-pirates. This rowdy crew soon grew restless, demanding that Kidd seize a prize ship soon.

Instead of seeking out pirates in the island havens around Madagascar, Kidd sailed to the Red Sea, the goal of a fleet of ships that each year carried gold, jewels, cloth, and other valuables from India's immensely wealthy Mogul empire to the Middle East. These ships were as tempting to pirates as the Spanish treasure fleets had been to the buccaneers of the Caribbean—but they were not among the ships Kidd was licensed to capture. By making this move, says Robert C. Ritchie, a historian at the University of California at San Diego who has written a biography of Kidd, "he was all but announcing he had turned pirate." [38]

Kidd Turns Pirate

When the Indian fleet arrived in mid-August of 1697, Kidd sailed close to one of the merchant ships and began firing at it, flying the red flag of a pirate. A British navy ship guarding the fleet chased the *Adventure Galley* away. Rumors calling Kidd a pirate had already begun to circulate along the Indian coast, and the navy captain's report added to this growing reputation. Robert Ritchie says that Kidd did not really deserve the pirate label, however, until later in August, when he captured a small trading ship near India. The ship flew an English flag and had an English captain, so it was completely off-limits to an English privateer.

After that the black marks against Kidd's name, though still fairly minor, mounted quickly. He damaged a Portuguese ship and ill-treated the natives of some islands where his ship stopped. Representatives of the British East India Company, very concerned about the damage that pirates were doing to their trading relationship with India, exaggerated these stories. Soon many people believed that William Kidd was one of the worst pirates in the Indian Ocean.

The Death of William Moore

Kidd's crew, meanwhile, was just as unhappy with him as the British and Indian merchants were, but for opposite reasons. Like William Dampier, Kidd apparently was a bad-tempered but ineffective commander, inspiring fear without respect. His crew disliked his threats of violence and his bragging about his noble friends. Most of all they disliked the fact that he had not yet captured any valuable prizes.

The *Adventure Galley*'s gunner, William Moore, was one of the worst complainers. On October 30, Kidd and Moore argued about whether to attack a nearby Dutch ship. "You have brought me to ruin and many more,"[39] Moore insisted. Furious, Kidd picked up a heavy wooden bucket and hit Moore on the head. The gunner fell to the deck, crying, "Farewell, farewell, Captain Kidd has given me my

Wielding a wooden bucket, Kidd dashes William Moore on the head. Moore died one day later.

last." [40] A day later he died of a fractured skull. Crew members later testified that Kidd seemed unconcerned, saying, "I have good friends in England that will bring me off [see that I am not charged] for that." [41]

In November, Kidd and his crew captured a small ship called the *Rupparell*. By flying a French flag, Kidd tricked the ship's British captain into revealing that the *Rupparell* had a French pass (passport), even though its owners and most of its officers were Dutch. Merchant ships in those days often carried flags and passports from several different countries to protect themselves from privateers. Because his privateering commission allowed him to attack French ships, Kidd claimed later that the French pass made the *Rupparell* his legal prey. In the next two months, however, he captured two more small ships that did not have French passes. None of these ships carried much of value, though they provided the *Adventure Galley* with some much-needed supplies.

A Rich Prize

Finally, on January 30, 1698, William Kidd's luck seemed to change. A huge ship called the *Quedah Merchant* came into view. It was riding low in the water, which meant that it was full of cargo, and it was traveling by itself. Again Kidd hoisted a French flag onto the *Adventure Galley*'s mast. The merchant ship replied with a similar flag, suggesting to Kidd that it would be a legal prize. His crew captured it easily, and it proved to contain just the kind of booty they had been dreaming of: rich silks and other fabrics, sugar, guns, jewels, and a considerable sum in gold and silver.

In fact, however, taking that particular ship was about as lucky as putting a hand into a hornet's nest. The *Quedah Merchant*, like the *Rupparell*, had a French pass, but it also had an English captain. Worse still, its owners included some of the most powerful men in the Great Mogul's court. They demanded that the East India Company make sure that this terrible pirate was caught. The company, in turn, pressured the British government to do something about Kidd.

Meanwhile, in April 1698, the *Adventure Galley*, with the *Quedah Merchant* and the *Rupparell* in tow, arrived at St. Mary's Island, a small island off the northeastern coast of Madagascar that was a well-known pirate haven. Kidd's crew could divide and sell the *Quedah Merchant*'s cargo there. They could also find a safe harbor for the *Adventure Galley*, which was leaking so badly that they had to pump water out of it night and day to keep it afloat.

Another pirate ship was already in the harbor. Its captain proved to be Robert Culliford, one of the men who had run away with the

Kidd watches as his friends stash his captured treasure for safekeeping.

Blessed William many years before. Kidd must have had mixed feelings about seeing his old shipmate again. Some of Kidd's crew later testified, however, that he reassured Culliford's men that "he was as bad as they."[42]

Keeping forty shares of the booty to take back to his investors, Kidd divided the rest of the *Quedah Merchant's* cargo among his crew. Most of his men then left him and joined Culliford. The *Adventure Galley* was beyond repair, so Kidd ran it up onto the beach and burned it.

A Wanted Man

Kidd left St. Mary's in November in the only more or less seaworthy ship he had left, the ungainly *Quedah Merchant,* now renamed the *Adventure Prize,* with the handful of sailors who were still loyal to him. He headed back to the Caribbean, reaching the island of Anguilla, a British possession, in early April 1699. There, to his horror, he learned that the British government had ordered all colonial governors to arrest him on sight.

Kidd apparently believed that the whole thing was a terrible misunderstanding. He had the French passes from the *Rupparell* and the *Quedah Merchant,* which proved—in his eyes—that he had done nothing illegal. He was sure that if he showed them to Lord Bellomont and explained what had happened, Bellomont and the Whig nobles in England could clear his name or, at least, obtain a pardon for him. On Hispaniola he exchanged the *Adventure Prize* for a more seaworthy sloop, the *Saint Antonio.* He sailed this ship to New York, where he hoped to find Bellomont, now the colony's governor.

Kidd reached New York in early June and eagerly greeted his wife and two stepdaughters. Learning that Bellomont was in Boston, the capital of the other colony he governed, the captain wrote to him at once, giving his version of events during his now-infamous voyage. He enclosed the French passes from the *Rupparell* and the *Quedah Merchant,* the only two ships he admitted capturing. He promised to go to Boston and give himself up if Bellomont would arrange a pardon for him and his remaining crewmen. At the same time, perhaps not completely trusting Bellomont, Kidd gave the valuables he had brought with him to several friends for safekeeping.

Betrayal

Bellomont proved to be anything but the rescuer Kidd was hoping for. The governor may have genuinely wanted to capture this man who seemed to have gone bad, or he may have feared that trying to help Kidd would damage his political position. In any case, he decided to betray Kidd. He wrote the captain a soothing letter, assuring him that all would be well, but when Kidd came to Boston in July, Bellomont had him arrested.

Kidd remained in a Boston prison for eight months. If he believed that his noble backers in Britain would help him, he was doomed to disappointment. The Whigs were starting to lose power in Parliament and their opponents, the conservative Tory Party, were looking for scandals to speed their fall. The East India Company was also no friend of the Whigs, who had limited its power. When the story of the Whig leaders' involvement with Kidd leaked out, both the Tories and the merchants were eager to make the most of it.

To avoid these attacks, the Whigs tried to separate themselves from the "obnoxious pirate"[43] Kidd and his actions. "Parliaments are grown into the habit of finding fault," one noted. Referring to the Bible story about a sailor who was thrown overboard as a sacrifice in the hope of calming a terrible storm and saving his shipmates, the Whig lord added, "Some Jonah or other must be thrown overboard, if the storm cannot otherwise be laid [calmed]."[44] The Whigs saw William Kidd as the ideal person for that unhappy role.

Trial of an "Obnoxious Pirate"

At the time, British pirates could be put on trial only in England, so Kidd was taken there in April 1700. By then he was ill and depressed. The Admiralty Board interviewed him, then put him in a filthy cell in London's Newgate Prison. He spent about a year there, during which he was allowed almost no visitors.

Considering possible impeachment of the Whig lords on the grounds of having aided a pirate, members of Parliament questioned Kidd in private sessions on March 27 and 31, 1701. He continued to insist on his innocence and refused to accuse his backers of any wrongdoing, though he was told that his life would be spared if he did so. The Tories failed to gain enough votes to impeach the Whigs, but the legislators apparently were not impressed with Kidd, either. One commented after the second hearing, "I thought him only a knave [criminal]. I now know him to be a fool as well." [45]

Kidd's trial took place on May 8 and 9. Typically for the time, he was notified of his trial date only two weeks before it arrived, and he was not given a defense attorney. He had to prepare his own defense and do his own cross-examination of witnesses. The chief proofs of his innocence that he hoped to be able to offer were the two French passes, which Bellomont was supposed to have sent to England, but Admiralty officials said they could not find them. No one probably will ever know whether they were genuinely mislaid or kept from Kidd deliberately. Some historians think that they would not have cleared him in any case because he had also seized other ships.

Kidd was tried first for killing William Moore. *The Adventure Galley's* surgeon and another crew member testified against Kidd in return for pardons. Kidd did not deny that he had hit Moore, but he insisted that "it was not designedly done but in my passion, for which I am heartily sorry." [46] He tried to establish during his cross-examination that he "had all the provocation in the world" [47] to strike Moore because Moore had insulted him and threatened mutiny. The two crewmen denied it, and the jury apparently did not believe other crewmen whom Kidd called to support his side of the story. After deliberating for only an hour, the jury found Kidd guilty of murder. The next day they made even shorter work of the piracy charges, finding Kidd guilty after just half an hour.

As both a murderer and a pirate, Kidd was sentenced to hang. When the judge asked him if he could give any reason why the sentence should not be carried out, Kidd said, "I am the innocentest person of them all, only I have been sworn against by perjured persons." [48]

The British Admiralty court convicts Kidd for murder and piracy.

Kidd's Execution

Kidd's execution took place on May 23, 1701, in a run-down district of London called Wapping. The execution of a pirate, especially such a famous one as Kidd had become, was both a solemn ceremony and a public spectacle. Kidd, along with several other pirates who were scheduled to hang, was paraded through the streets in an open cart. An official carrying a silver oar, representing the authority of the Admiralty, rode ahead of them in a carriage. A laughing, screaming crowd who saw the execution as a kind of holiday accompanied this grim procession. The parade ended at Execution Dock, where a gallows, or gibbet, was set up in the slimy mud lining the Thames River.

Kidd's last bit of good luck came in the form of a bottle. Some sympathetic person had given him liquor, and by the time he reached the gallows he was so drunk that he could hardly stand. Nonetheless, he made a rambling speech proclaiming his innocence and denouncing the powerful men who had betrayed him. His bad luck, however, lasted right to the end of his life. When the executioner first tried to hang him, the rope broke, dumping him in the mud. The process had to be repeated. This time, the rope held.

That was the end of the story for William Kidd. It was not, however, the end of the grisly ceremony of his execution. As was traditional after pirate executions, his body was left chained to a post at the water's edge until three tides had washed over it. It was then coated with tar and hung in a cage of iron bands that held the body together as it rotted. Only the most infamous pirates suffered this final indignity of "hanging in chains." Their bodies were displayed at the entrance to ports to show other sailors what would happen to them if they became pirates. Kidd's body remained on display at Tilbury Point, near London, for almost two years.

Chained and caged in iron bands, Kidd's body hung at Tilbury Point, near London, to warn sailors of the consequences of piracy.

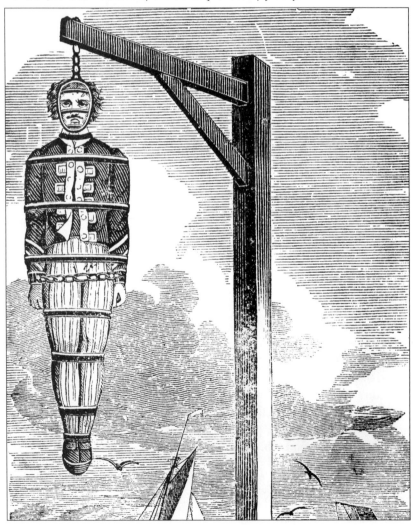

A Reputation Lives On

Kidd's death was also not the end of his reputation as an arch-pirate. Ballads and broadsheets, the equivalent of today's tabloid newspapers, described his supposed deeds in gory—and highly inaccurate—detail. Furthermore, his attempts to hide some of the spoils from the *Quedah Merchant* with his friends in New York spawned endless tales of fabulous buried treasure, which in turn led to numerous attempts to dig it up. None of these attempts, which have continued into modern times, uncovered anything significant—probably because there is nothing to uncover. Soon after Kidd was arrested, Lord Bellomont took steps to recover the items Kidd had stored, and most historians think he found all of them. Caught up in a changing political climate that was turning against pirates, William Kidd seems to have left little legacy except the story of his bad luck.

CHAPTER 5

Edward Teach (Blackbeard): The Fearsome Pirate

Blackbeard (as almost everyone called him) knew a lot about creating terror. He knew that terror came not so much from what he did as from what he could make people think he *might* do. If he made his appearance frightening enough, he would seldom have to prove his strength in a fight. Merchant captains would surrender simply at the sight of him, and no member of his crew would dare to disobey him. Blackbeard's terror tactics worked so well that he had a moderately successful pirate career without, as far as is documented, actually killing anyone until the day of his own death.

A giant of a man with dark, curly hair, Blackbeard would have been an impressive figure even without trying. During his years as a pirate, however, he built on his natural appearance to make himself as fearsome-looking as possible. In his *General History,* Charles Johnson described Blackbeard this way:

> Captain Teach assumed the cognomen [nickname] of Blackbeard, from that large quantity of hair, which, like a frightful meteor, covered his whole face, and frightened America more than any comet that has appeared there [in] a long time. This beard was black, which he suffered [allowed] to grow of an extravagant length; as to breadth, it came up to his eyes; he was accustomed to twist it with ribbons, in small tails, . . . and turn them about his ears: In time of action, he wore a sling over his shoulders, with three brace [pairs] of pistols, hanging in holsters . . . ; and stuck lighted matches [slow-burning, twisted strings of cotton] under his hat, which appearing on each side of his face, his eyes naturally looking fierce and wild, made him altogether such a figure, that imagination cannot form an idea of a fury, from hell, to look more frightful.[49]

Training of a Pirate

As with most pirates, Blackbeard's early years are obscure. Most historians believe that he was born in Bristol, England, around 1680. As a pirate he used the name Edward Teach, or Thatch (the name was spelled in a variety of ways), but he may have been born with a different name and used an alias to keep from shaming his family. He could read and write, which was usual only for people of the middle or upper class, so his parents may have been well-off. Like Henry Morgan, he proved able to get along well with members of high society as well as with hardened buccaneers.

Edward Teach, known as Blackbeard, invoked fear in all sailors that crossed his path.

Teach probably served as a privateer sponsored by Jamaica during "Queen Anne's War" in the early 1700s. No historical records of this period mention him, but Johnson said that he "distinguished himself for his uncommon boldness and personal courage." [50]

Like many other privateers, Teach was left unemployed when the Treaty of Utrecht ended the war in 1713. Shortly afterward he apparently moved from Jamaica to the pirate haven of Nassau. He joined the crew of veteran pirate Benjamin Hornigold late in 1716.

When Hornigold's pirates captured a large, sturdy French merchant ship called the *Concorde* in 1717, Hornigold gave the ship to Teach as a reward. Teach remodeled it and, perhaps remembering his earlier privateering service, renamed it *Queen Anne's Revenge*. This vessel, which carried forty cannons and a crew of three hundred, was as much a giant among pirate ships as its captain was a giant among men.

Building a Reputation

Soon after Teach took control of the *Queen Anne's Revenge*, he and Hornigold separated. Now on his own as a pirate, Teach worked hard to build a ferocious reputation. He grew the long, bushy black beard that was to make him famous and began using the name Blackbeard. He often dressed all in black as well. He also behaved in ways that made sure people would remember him. For instance, one night in a tavern he mixed gunpowder into his rum, set the explosive mixture on fire, and then drank it.

He spread the story that the *Queen Anne's Revenge* had fought with a British navy ship, the *Scarborough,* and made the warship back away. Johnson and some later historians accepted this feat as a fact, but others say there is no evidence that the battle ever took place.

Blackbeard commuted between the Caribbean and southeastern North America, seizing ships in both places. He came to concentrate on North Carolina, the only North American colony where pirates were still welcome. Dotted with small islands, narrow inlets, and sandbars among which a pirate ship could hide and a large navy ship could not follow, North Carolina's coastal geography made it an ideal pirate haven. The colony encouraged pirates because, unlike other North American colonies at the time, it had few resources that it could sell in legitimate trade.

In January 1718, Blackbeard accepted the king's pardon from North Carolina's governor, Charles Eden. He promised to give up piracy, but if he ever meant to keep this promise, he soon changed his mind. Two months later he was out cruising again.

The Gentleman Pirate

While in the Bay of Honduras, off Central America, Blackbeard met another pirate who was in many ways his exact opposite: Major Stede Bonnet, later often called "the gentleman pirate." Bonnet, a plump middle-aged man, had been an army officer and a wealthy sugar cane planter on the island of Barbados before he decided to become a pirate in 1717. No one knows why he made this sudden change in his life, though some stories claim that he left home to escape a bad-tempered wife.

Blackbeard quickly saw that Bonnet, unlike himself, knew very little about either sailing or commanding a crew. Something about Bonnet must have appealed to the more experienced pirate, however, because he suggested that the two of them sail together. Blackbeard put one of his own officers in charge of Bonnet's ship, the *Revenge*, and invited Bonnet to stay aboard the *Queen Anne's Revenge*. According to Johnson, Blackbeard politely urged Bonnet to relax and

Befriended by Blackbeard, Major Stede Bonnet has been called the gentleman pirate.

let someone else do the work of being captain. Polite or not, he did not really give Bonnet a chance to refuse. Bonnet remained essentially a well-treated prisoner on Blackbeard's ship for a little more than a year.

Terrible Stories

Blackbeard soon captured a third ship, the *Adventure*, and made it part of his growing fleet. After traveling among other islands, the three ships sailed back to the Bay of Honduras in early April 1718 and persuaded all the ships anchored there—one large vessel and four smaller ones—to surrender without a fight. By this time, Blackbeard's crew, now numbering about four hundred, was equally in awe of him. They apparently admired his seamanship and both respected and feared him. Johnson wrote that Blackbeard "might have pass'd in the world for a hero, had he been employ'd in a good cause." [51]

The stories that circulated about Blackbeard grew more terrible as time went on. There is no evidence to support tales that he mistreated prisoners, such as the story that he chopped off the finger of a man who refused to take off his ring. He apparently did abuse at least one crewman, however. One night while drinking with one of his officers, Israel Hands, and another man, Blackbeard stealthily took out two guns and held them under the table. The other man heard him cock the pistols and quietly left, but Hands remained unaware. Suddenly Blackbeard blew out the room's only candle, crossed his arms under the table, and fired both guns. The bullet from one struck Hands in the knee, crippling him for life. When asked why he had done such a thing, Blackbeard (according to Johnson) replied that "if he did not now and then kill one of them, they would forget who he was." [52]

The Blockade of Charleston

Near the end of May 1718, Blackbeard carried out what journalist Frank Sherry calls "one of the most audacious acts of piracy ever committed." [53] The *Queen Anne's Revenge,* accompanied by the *Revenge,* the *Adventure,* and another sloop, blockaded the harbor of Charleston, South Carolina, the most important port in the southern colonies. They stopped all vessels entering or leaving the harbor for several days, about nine in all. The pirates seized everything of value on the ships, including a group of leading Charleston citizens who became Blackbeard's hostages.

Blackbeard sent two of his officers and one captured passenger into Charleston. They told the colony's governor that Blackbeard had promised to kill all the hostages and set fire to the town unless his demands were met within two days. Amazingly, the only thing the pirate asked for was a chestful of medicines. No one knows why he wanted the medicines so badly or why he did not ask for money or other valuables as well.

The governor gave the pirates what they asked for, but bad weather delayed the messengers' return to the *Queen Anne's Revenge.* Fortunately, the hostages had been able to persuade Blackbeard to extend his deadline, and all were unharmed. With the medicine chest in hand, Blackbeard released his prisoners, although he kept all their possessions and even most of their clothes. He also returned the captured ships to their captains. He then departed with his loot.

Downsizing a Crew

Soon after the Charleston blockade, Blackbeard apparently decided that he no longer wanted to maintain a large pirate fleet. In early June he sailed his ships into an area called Topsail Inlet (now Beaufort

Inlet) in North Carolina and ran the *Queen Anne's Revenge* aground on a sandbank, probably on purpose. He arranged for the *Adventure* to be run aground as well. He left the *Revenge* behind for Stede Bonnet, whom he had persuaded to visit Governor Eden to obtain a pardon. Then he quietly loaded all the group's booty and his forty favorite crew members onto a small sloop that had been a supply ship for the three larger vessels and sailed away.

When other crew members discovered what was happening and protested against being cheated out of their share of the plunder, Blackbeard marooned twenty-five of them on a small, sandy island. They probably would have starved to death there if Bonnet had not discovered and rescued them on his return two days later. Bonnet and the angry crew members searched for Blackbeard for a while, but they never caught him.

A "Retired" Pirate

Blackbeard and his greatly reduced crew returned to the North Carolina port of Bath, where he took a second pardon from Governor Eden later in June. He apparently became friends with Eden and some of his officials as well as with the local planters. He entertained them and even married one of the planters' daughters, a sixteen-year-old girl whose name some sources give as Mary Ormond. Governor Eden

After being marooned by Blackbeard, one pirate sits in disgust on a deserted island.

Blackbeard's crew dances, drinks, and parties on the Carolina coast.

himself performed the ceremony. This was probably the pirate's only legal marriage, although he was said to have had at least thirteen other "wives" in various ports.

By September, Blackbeard had established a settlement near the southern tip of Ocracoke Island, a sandy island across Pamlico Sound from Bath. He anchored his ship nearby in Ocracoke Inlet. He made one voyage to the Caribbean from there, collecting a French ship near Bermuda. He claimed the ship as salvage, saying he had found it floating with no one on board. This unlikely, though not impossible, tale makes some historians suspect that he returned to piracy, at least briefly. For the most part, however, Blackbeard seemed willing to relax in his supposed retirement.

When Charles Vane, another well-known pirate captain, visited Blackbeard with his crew late in September, the sea rovers had a weeklong orgy of dancing, eating, and drinking, which Frank Sherry calls "one of the largest gatherings of pirates ever held." [54] Some people suspected that this meeting was more than just a giant party. Rumors began to circulate that Blackbeard was planning to turn Ocracoke Island into a fortified pirate base, "another Madagascar."

A Secret Expedition

Feeling that Governor Eden and his friends were entirely too friendly with Blackbeard, some North Carolina planters asked Alexander Spotswood, the governor of Virginia, for help in controlling the pirate. Although he had no legal right to interfere in the affairs of his neighboring colony, Spotswood was happy to oblige. "I judged it high time to destroy that crew of villains, and not to suffer [allow] them to gather strength in the neighborhood of so valuable a trade as that of this colony,"[55] he wrote to the Council of Trade and Plantations in London.

Spotswood set up a secret expedition to destroy Blackbeard. He bought two small sloops with his own money and persuaded the captains of the *Pearl* and the *Lyme*, two British warships stationed in Virginia, to provide fifty-five sailors to man them. (The warships themselves were much too large to enter the shallow waters around Blackbeard's hideout.) He offered the men a reward for each pirate they captured or killed. Lieutenant Robert Maynard, an officer on the *Pearl*, agreed to lead the expedition.

The Battle of Ocracoke Inlet

The two sloops, the *Jane* and the *Ranger*, reached Ocracoke Inlet around sunset on November 21, 1718. A short distance away, Blackbeard was drinking aboard his ship with a visiting trader and some of his crew. Only about twenty men were with him at the time. He apparently either did not see the navy vessels or felt sure that they could not harm him.

Early the next morning, Maynard sent a rowboat to scout out the path to Blackbeard's ship among the treacherous sandbars. Blackbeard fired at the boat, then cut his ship's anchor cable and began heading for the island. He probably hoped to slip into a narrow channel on the other side of a sandbar and escape through it to the open sea.

As Blackbeard's ship and the navy sloops drew closer together, they began firing at each other. Blackbeard lifted his drinking cup and saluted his attackers, saying, "Damnation seize my soul if I give you quarters [mercy], or take any from you."[56] Maynard replied that he, too, would neither give nor expect mercy.

When the two sloops temporarily ran aground on a sandbar, Blackbeard fired his ship's eight cannons at them, raking them with a deadly rain of metal pellets, nails, and scraps of iron. The broadside badly damaged the *Ranger* and killed nine men aboard it, including the ship's captain and officers, so it had to withdraw from the battle. Twenty members of the *Jane*'s crew were wounded or killed as well. With great effort, however, Maynard worked his sloop free of the sandbar and headed for the pirate ship once more. He told most of his unwounded men to hide below the *Jane*'s deck, fully armed with swords and pistols, and wait for his signal.

Seeing only a few men on Maynard's sloop, Blackbeard shouted to his crew, "They were all knocked on the head except three or four.

Blackbeard and his crew charge onto Jane's *deck. There they confront Lieutenant Robert Maynard's well armed men.*

Let's jump on board, and cut them to pieces!"⁵⁷ As the two ships touched, Blackbeard and about ten other pirates leaped across to the sloop. Maynard then cried out to his own sailors, who poured onto the *Jane's* deck, yelling and firing their guns. The deck quickly became slippery with blood as pirates and navy men fought hand to hand.

Fall of a Giant

Soon Blackbeard and Maynard were face-to-face. Each fired a gun at the other. Blackbeard's shot missed. Maynard's did not, but having a bullet in his body did not seem to disturb the giant pirate. The two fought on, now using swords. Finally Blackbeard broke Maynard's sword and moved in to give the navy captain the killing stroke. Before he could do so, however, one of Maynard's men struck him in the throat with another sword. Others attacked as well. Blackbeard finally collapsed after five bullets and some twenty knife thrusts had torn through his body.

Maynard, who had received only a minor wound on one hand, cut off Blackbeard's head and hung it on the front of his sloop. He then threw the pirate's body overboard. Given how hard Blackbeard had been to kill, it was no wonder that the story soon circulated that his headless corpse had swum around Maynard's ship three times before sinking.

Seeing their leader dead, most of the remaining pirates surrendered or jumped overboard. One, however, a loyal African ex-slave named Caesar, tried to set fire to the pirate ship's gunpowder supply. He planned to blow up pirates and attackers together, as he had apparently promised Blackbeard he would do in such a desperate situation. Two men from a captured merchant vessel, prisoners aboard Blackbeard's ship, forcibly stopped him.

Missing Treasure

Maynard stopped at Ocracoke Island in the hope of finding the loot Blackbeard had kept from the siege of Charleston and other raids. He located twenty-five barrels of sugar, eleven of cocoa, one of indigo (a valuable blue dye), and a bale of cotton—but no gold, silver, or jewels.

Johnson said Blackbeard had hinted that there was more. The night before the pirate leader was killed, some of his crew supposedly asked him whether his wife knew where his money was hidden in case anything should happen to him. He replied that "nobody but himself and the Devil knew where it was, and the longest liver should take all." [58] Many hopeful treasure hunters have searched for Blackbeard's booty since then, but as with Captain Kidd's fabled treasure, no one has found anything. Most historians believe that there is nothing to find. In spite of his awe-inspiring reputation, Blackbeard captured only about twenty ships during his short career, and none of these carried very valuable cargo.

After a face-to-face duel with Maynard, Blackbeard lies mortally wounded on the Jane's *deck.*

With his grisly trophy and the remains of both his own crew and Blackbeard's, Maynard finally made his way back to Virginia. Fifteen of Blackbeard's pirates were tried in Williamsburg on March 12, 1719, and thirteen of them were hanged soon afterward. In *Jolly Roger,* his history of the golden age pirates, Patrick Pringle writes that the death of Blackbeard, the fearsome pirate, and his men marked "virtually the end of [North] American piracy."[59]

CHAPTER 6

Anne Bonny: The Woman Pirate

Anne Bonny was not a pirate leader, yet she and her shipmate Mary Read have achieved lasting fame—because they were women. Most of Bonny's life story is known only from the account in Johnson's *General History,* and Johnson may have invented part of it. Johnson himself admitted that "some may be tempted to think the whole story no better than a novel or romance." [60] Still, there is no question that Bonny and Read were real, and Tamara J. Eastman, a teacher in Virginia who has researched Bonny's life extensively, says she has found evidence that supports at least the basic facts that Johnson reported.

Anne Bonny achieved lasting fame as one of the only women pirates.

According to Eastman, Anne Bonny was born in 1698 in Kinsale, County Cork, Ireland. She was the illegitimate child of William Cormac, a married attorney, and Mary Brennan, a maid who worked in his family's household. The affair became a public scandal, and local people stopped bringing their legal business to Cormac. Cormac, Brennan, and young Anne therefore left Ireland to begin a new life in the American colony of Carolina. (North and South Carolina did not separate until 1712.)

A New Beginning

William Cormac and his second family did better in their new home. Cormac became a merchant and eventually grew rich enough to buy a large rice plantation. According to Johnson and Eastman, the Cormacs were soon counted among the families who ruled Charleston society. The only sad note was Brennan's death in 1711, when Anne was thirteen years old.

Anne, as the child of a wealthy planter, would have been raised to lead a quiet life. Such a life did not suit her, Johnson wrote. She was reported to have a "fierce and courageous" [61] temper. Some people said that she once stabbed a servant girl to death. Others claimed that when a young man tried to attack her, she hurt him so badly that he was bedridden for several weeks. Johnson doubted these tales, but they showed what acquaintances thought Anne was capable of doing.

John Rackham, known as Calico Jack, first introduced Bonny to the pirate lifestyle.

Meeting the Pirates

In 1718, when she was about twenty years old, Anne married a poor sailor and fisherman named James Bonny. Johnson claimed that Anne's father, furious about what he saw as an unsuitable match, cut her out of his will and turned her out of his household.

Looking for work, the Bonnys moved to Nassau, the pirate haven in the Bahamas. Anne met the pirates and found that she enjoyed their company, especially that of a dashing captain named John Rackham. Rackham was nicknamed Calico Jack because he liked to wear striped pants made of lightweight cotton material called calico. Pirate expert David Cordingly says that Rackham was "a small-time pirate," [62] attacking mostly fishing boats and small trading ships in the seas around the Bahamas.

Bonny, who apparently did not take marriage vows any more seriously than her father had, left her husband and went to sea with Rackham in 1719. During her first days aboard Rackham's ship, she pretended to be a man, but the other crew members probably learned her secret before long. Most pirate ships' articles forbade having women on board, but the crewmen most likely came to respect Bonny when they saw that she worked and fought as hard as any of them.

A Surprising Story

Rackham captured several small prize vessels after Bonny joined him. One, taken in the summer of 1720, was a Dutch merchant ship whose crew proved to include one British member, a handsome, beardless youth whose name supposedly was Mark Read. Read joined the pirates, and Bonny found herself attracted to the young sailor. As Johnson told it, Bonny, in a quiet moment alone with Read, re-

Mary Read (pictured here) forged an instant friendship with Bonny in the male-dominated pirate life.

vealed that she was a woman—and was thunderstruck when Read did the same. Her real first name, she said, was Mary.

Not surprisingly, Bonny and Read, alone in a man's world, became close friends. At first they kept Read's true identity hidden. After Calico Jack became jealous and threatened to kill what appeared to be Bonny's new boyfriend, however, they let him in on the secret.

During their days at sea together, Anne Bonny and Mary Read no doubt told each other their life stories. Read's past, at least as Johnson described it, had been even more adventurous than Bonny's. Like Bonny, Read, born in England, was illegitimate, but she had never known the comforts of Bonny's later childhood. Her mother had married a sailor and had a son by him, but the sailor died or deserted the family soon after the boy's birth. Mary, born about a year later, had a different father, who did not marry her mother.

After a few years, Mary's mother ran out of money. She asked the sailor's mother, who was fairly well-to-do, for funds to help in raising the woman's grandson. To hide the fact that the little boy had actually died in infancy, Mary's mother dressed her in boy's clothes and tried to pass her off as her brother. The trick worked, and it apparently gave Mary a taste for dressing in males' clothing that she never lost. After the grandmother died, Mary and her mother were desperate for money once more, so Mary became a "footboy" (junior servant) to a Frenchwoman at age thirteen.

Adventures in Disguise

Wanting a more adventurous life, Read—still in disguise as a male—soon joined the crew of a warship and then, returning to land, became a soldier. According to Johnson, she "behaved herself with a great deal of bravery" [63] in action. After awhile she fell in love with another soldier and let him discover her secret. He returned her affection, and she insisted that they marry as soon as possible. The marriage took place as soon as the regiment moved into its winter quarters.

Several officers of the regiment, startled but perhaps amused at this unusual love story, gave the couple money to set up a household. The newlyweds arranged to be discharged from the military and settled in Holland, where they bought a tavern called the Three Horseshoes. Unfortunately, Read's husband died after a few years, and business fell off, so she sold the tavern. She returned, first to the military life, and then to sea aboard the Dutch merchant ship on which Rackham had found her.

Some modern experts have found Read's story even harder to believe than Bonny's. It would have been difficult or impossible, they say, for a woman to conceal her sex for as long as Read supposedly did while living with groups of men under the extremely crude conditions that existed aboard a ship or in a military camp in the early eighteenth century. However, David Cordingly points out that there were several proven cases, both during and after Read's time, in which adventurous women did precisely that. "The history of the Royal [British] Navy and the merchant service is littered with examples of women who successfully dressed as men and worked alongside them for years on end without being discovered," [64] he writes. Very few women took the final step of becoming pirates, however, and no others achieved fame during the era in which Bonny and Read lived.

Fierce Fighters

On board the pirate ship, Bonny and Read worked and fought side by side. Their identity as women was no longer hidden. According to testimony at their trial, they wore women's clothes aboard ship except during battles, when they changed to the more practical men's clothing. The men learned to treat them with respect, both because they did their share of the work—Bonny, for instance, brought gunpowder to the crew members during one battle with another ship—and because they proved quite able to protect themselves. At their trial, Johnson reported, men who had served with them testified that "in times of action, no person amongst them were more resolute, or ready to board [prize ships] or undertake any thing that was hazardous, as [Mary Read] and Anne Bonny." [65]

In the months after Read joined the crew, Rackham's ship captured several small vessels. These acts of piracy drew the attention of the Bahamas' new governor, Woodes Rogers, who was trying to clean the pirates out of the islands. He issued an order for the arrest of Rackham's crew in September 1720, listing known members, including both Bonny and Read, by name. He sent two sloops out to look for them.

On the night of October 22, Jonathan Barnett, the captain of one of these sloops, spotted Rackham's ship in Dry Harbor Bay, near the western tip of the island. The pirates had been celebrating the taking of a prize ship the previous day, and most of them were drunk. As a result, Barnett's ship was able to come quite close before anyone on the pirate ship spotted it. When Barnett called out to the anchored ship and asked the captain to identify himself, Rackham boldly gave his real name. Barnett then ordered Rackham to surrender, but the pirate fired one of his ship's guns at Barnett's sloop in response. Rackham's shot missed, but Barnett's return fire disabled the pirate ship.

Jonathan Barnett's ship exchanges cannon fire with Calico Jack's ship in a fierce battle.

Most of the pirates gave up at that point and tried to hide in the interior of the ship. Even Calico Jack offered to surrender. Barnett reported later, however, that three of the pirates refused to stop fighting, and two of them were Anne Bonny and Mary Read. Screaming and swearing, they fired their pistols at the invaders. They shouted equally loudly at their fellow crew members to come out and fight. Indeed, Johnson claimed that Mary Read fired her gun into the ship's hold where the men were cowering, killing one and wounding others.

Pirates on Trial

Resisting or not, all the pirates were quickly captured and taken to Jamaica to be tried. Rackham and his men were put on trial on November 16 and 17. The twelve judges found the men guilty and sentenced them to be hanged. Johnson wrote that on November 18, the day of his execution, Calico Jack asked to visit Bonny one last time and was given his wish. Instead of bidding him a tearful farewell, however, Bonny said only that "she was sorry to see him there, but if he had fought like a man, he need not have been hang'd like a dog." [66]

Bonny and Read had a separate trial, with the same judges, on November 28. They were accused of committing four acts of piracy in September and October, during which they had stolen a variety of gear from several ships and put their crews "in . . . fear of their lives." [67]

Several people who had been aboard the plundered ships testified that the two women "did not seem to be kept . . . by force, but of their own free-will and consent." [68] They said they had seen both women taking active parts in the pirate attacks. Dorothy Thomas, whom Rackham's pirates had captured in her canoe on the north side of Jamaica, said that Bonny and Read "wore men's jackets, and long trousers, and handkerchiefs tied about their heads; and that each of them had a machet [machete, a large knife] and pistol in their hands, and cursed and swore at the men," [69] telling them to kill Thomas so that she could not be a witness against them.

"We Plead Our Bellies"

Bonny and Read pled not guilty, but they offered no witnesses or evidence in their defense. Not surprisingly, the commissioners convicted them. Only then did the two women present an unbreakable defense, not against the charges of piracy but against the death sentence: "Milord, we plead our bellies." [70] In other words, both women claimed to be pregnant. British law stated that a woman could not be put to death while she was carrying a child because doing so would kill her

72

Bonny (left) and Read remain the most notorious women pirates.

unborn baby, which was innocent of any crime. The governor ordered the sentence to be postponed if an examination verified their claim, which it did.

Unlike Calico Jack, Anne Bonny and Mary Read never did hang. Read reportedly died of a fever, or possibly in childbirth, while she was still in prison. Bonny's fate is less clear. Johnson wrote that friends of her father's on Jamaica recognized her, and Tamara Eastman believes that Bonny's father himself may have helped to rescue his rebellious daughter in the summer of 1721. He could have bribed the Jamaican governor to have her quietly released, then taken her back to Charleston under an assumed name.

In *The Pirate Trial of Anne Bonny and Mary Read,* Eastman writes that some papers in the possession of William Cormac's descendants indicate (though they do not absolutely prove) that Bonny was married to a man from Virginia in December 1721. Eastman thinks that Bonny's father may have arranged the marriage to help his daughter assume a new identity. If so, the effort was successful, for Bonny's name never appeared in criminal or historical records again. She lived on only in people's imaginations.

CHAPTER 7

Bartholomew Roberts: The Successful Pirate

If ever a real pirate came close to fitting the romantic image of a pirate leader, it was surely Bartholomew Roberts. He was tall, with dark hair and eyes, for which he gained the nickname "Black Bart." According to some reports, he was handsome. He and his crew dressed as colorfully as any pirate in a movie or play. He said he wanted to live "a merry life and a short one" [71]—and he did.

If ever a pirate could be considered successful at his work, that, too, was Bartholomew Roberts. Most pirates were lucky to capture ten or twenty ships during their careers. During the three years Black Bart was a pirate, however, he and his crew took more than four hundred ships. Although few people know his name today, Roberts in his own time was called "the Great Pirate"—and for good reason. For a brief time he all but brought shipping in the Caribbean to a halt. His very name terrorized captains from Newfoundland to West Africa. The sight of his black flag, with its white skull and cutlass, made most of them give up without firing a shot. Marine historian David Cordingly writes, "It is curious that Bartholomew Roberts has never acquired the fame of Blackbeard or Captain Kidd, because he was infinitely more successful than either of them, and was a considerably more attractive figure." [72]

Becoming a Pirate

Black Bart did not start his sailing career on the wrong side of the law. He did not start it as Bartholomew, either. Like Henry Morgan, he came from Wales. He was born around 1682 in a little village called Casnewydd Bach, which means Little Newcastle in Welsh. His name then was John Roberts. He changed his first name to Bartholomew soon after he became a pirate; no one knows why.

Roberts apparently went to sea as a boy. By 1719, he was thirty-seven years old and an experienced sailor. He was second mate on the *Princess,* a merchant ship licensed by the Royal African Company, which controlled all of Britain's trade in slaves, to carry "black ivory" from West Africa to the Americas. Around June 5, the *Princess* was in the area then called the Gold Coast, picking up a new load of human cargo, when two ships flying black flags swooped down on it and two other ships. All three merchant ships hauled down their flags in surrender and let the pirates board them.

When the captured ships' officers were taken aboard the pirate ship and asked if they wanted to join its crew, Roberts at first refused. After a few days on the ship, however, he changed his mind. He may

Bartholomew Roberts, known as Black Bart, was the most successful pirate to ever sail. He captured more than four hundred ships in three years.

have liked the group's leader, a cheerful fellow Welshman named Howell Davis, and enjoyed the pirates' free way of life. According to Charles Johnson's *General History*, Roberts later said that he had joined the pirates "to get rid of the disagreeable superiority of some masters [captains] he was acquainted with, and [because of] the love of novelty and change."[73]

A New Leader

Just a few weeks later, Davis was killed in an ambush. The most experienced members of his crew then met to choose a new leader. In mockery of the British Parliament, this group called themselves the

A Portuguese soldier stabs Captain Howell Davis (foreground) in an ambush shortly after Black Bart joined Davis's crew. Black Bart is chosen as the new leader.

House of Lords, the name given to Parliament's upper house (the equivalent of the Senate in the United States). Amazingly, the "lords" chose Bartholomew Roberts, even though he had been with the pirates a very short time. Johnson wrote that a pirate named Dennis recommended Roberts in these words:

> It is my advice, that . . . we pitch upon [choose] a man of courage, and skill'd in navigation, one, who by his council [advice] and bravery seems best able to defend this commonwealth [the pirate group], and ward [protect] us from the dangers and tempests of an instable [undependable] element [the sea], and the fatal consequences of anarchy [complete lack of government]; and such a one I take Roberts to be. A fellow, I think, in all respects, worthy [of] your esteem and favor.[74]

Roberts accepted the position, saying, Johnson reported, that "since he had dipp'd his hands in muddy water [voluntarily taken part in criminal acts], and must be a pirate, it was better being a commander than a common man."[75] He knew that keeping his command would be a challenge, however. When urging his fellow crew members to choose Roberts, Dennis had reminded them that they could always depose or even kill him if they did not like him.

A Bold Attack

After capturing several ships off West Africa, Roberts and the House of Lords decided to sail across the Atlantic to Brazil, on the eastern coast of South America. Several weeks of cruising there brought the pirates no prizes, however. They were just about to move on to the West Indies when, in September 1719, they discovered a fleet of forty-two Portuguese merchant ships and two warships anchored in Bahía de Todos os Santos (All Saints Bay). With the boldness that was to mark his entire career, Roberts sailed up to one of the largest merchant vessels and told its crew to send their captain to him in a boat, warning them that he would kill them and destroy their ship if they fought back or raised an alarm. When the captain arrived, Roberts asked him which vessel in the fleet held the richest cargo. The captain pointed to a ship called the *Sagrada Familia (Holy Family)*.

Although it was not a warship, the *Sagrada Familia* was well armed. With forty ship's guns and a crew of 150, it should have been able to defeat the pirates easily all by itself. That did not stop Roberts, however. He sailed up to the ship, fired a broadside, grappled it to his own

Rushing across a grapple, Black Bart's crew overwhelms the Portuguese sailors aboard the merchant vessel Sagrada Familia.

Rover, and sent his men pouring onto the merchant's deck. The Portuguese sailors fought back, but Roberts's crew soon overwhelmed them.

The other merchant ships fired their guns as a distress signal to the warships when they heard the fighting. By the time the warships got under way, however, the *Rover* had escorted the *Sagrada Familia*, now sailed by part of Roberts's crew, out of the bay. The ship proved to contain a valuable cargo of hides, sugar, and tobacco, as well as a small fortune in gold coins and a diamond-studded cross intended for the king of Portugal. In his pirate history, *Jolly Roger*, Patrick Pringle writes that "for sheer daring this seizure has no parallel in the history of piracy." [76]

Rules to Live By

The combination of bravery and success that marked this adventure cemented most of the crew's loyalty to Roberts. They concluded that he was "pistol proof" [77] and that they had much to gain by staying with him. "By a better management than usual," Johnson wrote, Roberts "became the chief director in every thing of moment [importance],"[78] even in this determinedly democratic crew. Johnson said that pirates usually chose for their captain "one superior for knowledge and boldness, . . . [who] can make those fear, who do not love him; Roberts [was] said to have exceeded his fellows in these respects."[79] Roberts also made sure of his power by keeping the House of Lords on his side, knowing that they in turn could control the other men.

Not everyone was convinced, however. About a month later Walter Kennedy, the pirates' second in command, whom Roberts had left in charge of the Portuguese prize, sailed away with the *Sagrada Familia* and its loot. Furious at this desertion, Roberts decided that his crew needed some new "rules to live by" if they were to keep the discipline necessary to succeed as pirates. He drew up a series of articles, which all the crew signed and swore on a Bible to obey.

Roberts's articles were a little more strict than those governing other pirate ships. Unlike most other pirates, Roberts drank little alcohol, and he tried to keep his men from drinking excessively on shipboard so that they would always be ready for action. He also banned activities that might cause arguments between crew members, such as gambling. Roberts's crew apparently recognized the wisdom of these restrictions and respected their captain enough to accept them, even though they somewhat limited the free pirate way of life.

Capturing a Harbor

Roberts and his crew next sailed into the Caribbean, where they took a number of prizes. Island governors sent privateer ships after him, causing battles that killed several pirates. Perhaps tired of being chased, Roberts decided to leave the West Indies for a while. He sailed up the eastern coast of North America to Newfoundland (now part of Canada), capturing an assortment of ships on the way. When the pirates' sloop reached the harbor of Trepassey in late June 1720, they sailed straight in "with their black colors [flag] flying, drums beating, and trumpets sounding," Johnson wrote.[80] Again, Roberts's boldness—and what was by now a reputation almost as fearsome as Blackbeard's—worked. The crews of all twenty-two ships in the harbor, some twelve hundred men, abandoned their vessels and headed for shore. Even the governor of New England, later sending an unhappy report of the raid to Britain, wrote, "One cannot withhold admiration for [Roberts's] bravery and daring."[81]

After plundering Trepassey and the nearby harbor of St. Mary's, the pirates sailed back down the New England coast, taking still more ships. They usually released captains and crews who surrendered without a fight, and Roberts even sometimes gave the captains their ships back after he and his men had removed what they wanted. For some reason the pirates were less kind to the cargoes, however. They often tore up or threw overboard any merchandise they did not want.

A Long, Thirsty Journey

Later in the summer of 1720, Roberts returned briefly to the West Indies. He then decided to head for the coast of West Africa, where slaves and the gold and goods that were traded for them were bound to make rich pickings. Unfortunately, the pirates made a mistake in their navigation, an easy thing to do in those days, and found themselves in a part of the ocean where winds kept them away from the African shore. They finally decided that they would have to head back across the Atlantic to the Caribbean.

The pirates were not prepared for a long journey across the open sea. They had only one barrel of drinking water—sixty-three gallons—to supply 124 men. Each man was soon limited to one mouthful of water a day, and after a while they could not have even that. Driven half insane by thirst and fever in the tropical heat, many of them died. The survivors were "as weak as it was possible for men to be and be alive,"[82] Johnson wrote, when they finally reached the Dutch colony of Surinam, on the northern coast of South America, and obtained fresh water at last. It was the first land they had seen in two thousand miles.

From the West Indies to Africa

Their health restored, the pirates settled down to terrorize the Caribbean once again. By the spring of 1721, they "had brought seaborne trade in the West Indies practically to a standstill,"[83] writes Stanley Richards, a biographer of Roberts. Roberts and his House of Lords decided they could trade their captured goods for gold more effectively and safely in Africa than in the Caribbean, so at the beginning of April the group set off for West Africa once more.

This time the pirates reached their destination, arriving at the mouth of the Senegal River in early June. During the rest of the year they captured ships at several African ports. By this time Roberts commanded a fleet of four pirate ships and a crew of 508 men.

Roberts had heard that two British warships, the *Swallow* and the *Weymouth*, were cruising the area in search of pirates. Bold as he was, Black Bart was not foolish enough to think he could win a battle with such heavily armed ships. Based on what he was told of the path the ships were expected to follow, however, he thought he could easily avoid them. He did not realize that the warships had had to change their sailing plans because of illness among their crews. The *Swallow*,

Black Bart's crew scales the side of an unsuspecting ship. His fleet of four ships and 508 men terrorized merchant ships, halting sea trade.

the larger of the two warships, in fact was much closer to the pirates than any of them dreamed.

A Clever Captain

Chaloner Ogle, the captain of the *Swallow*, caught up with Roberts at Cape Lopez, a maze of swamps and lagoons near the mouth of the Gabon River. Roberts had anchored there with his flagship, *Royal Fortune*, and two smaller ships, *Ranger* and *Little Ranger*. Ogle learned of their presence around dawn on February 5, 1722, when he heard a shot. He looked in the direction of the noise and spotted the pirates.

Roberts and his men saw the *Swallow*, too, but they did not recognize it for what it was. Thinking that the ship was a Portuguese trading vessel and guessing at its cargo, Roberts told James Skyrm, the captain of the *Ranger*, "There is . . . sugar in the offing, bring it in." [84]

At that moment, Ogle had to turn the *Swallow* away from the pirates to avoid the dangerously shallow water over a sandbank. The *Ranger*'s crew, thinking that the strange ship was fleeing from them, gave chase. Ogle guessed their mistake and decided to go on acting the part of a frightened merchant. He sailed farther out to sea, luring the *Ranger* away from the other pirate ships.

When Ogle had accomplished his aim, he let the *Ranger* draw close and then began raking it with the *Swallow*'s powerful guns. The startled pirates now realized what they were facing, but it was too late to run away, so they fired back. The battle went on until the pirate ship and its crew were so badly damaged that they had to surrender.

Placing the captured pirates under guard in the *Swallow*, Ogle went after Roberts and his other two ships. On the morning of February 10, he found them anchored with another vessel, the *Neptune*. Roberts's crew had captured the new ship just the day before, and the pirates had been celebrating all night. As a result, most of them were drunk or hungover. One of the few still sober was Roberts, who was in his cabin sharing a spicy stew called salmagundy—a favorite pirate dish—with the *Neptune*'s captain, Thomas Hill. When someone spotted the distant *Swallow*, the tipsy buccaneers idly debated whether it was Portuguese, French, or simply the *Ranger* coming back. Even Roberts did not pay much attention to the stranger until the *Swallow* came close enough for one pirate, a deserter from the British navy who happened to have served on that very warship, to recognize it.

Death of a Dashing Leader

Just as Roberts had always feared, drunkenness made many of his men unfit for duty just when he needed them the most. The loss of the *Ranger*'s crew also greatly reduced the group's strength. Nonetheless, the pirate captain did his best to get his miserable crew ready for battle. He rapidly considered several desperate plans, including escaping into the forest or even, if all else failed, grappling his ship to the *Swallow* and blowing them both up.

As the *Swallow* neared the *Royal Fortune*, Roberts jumped on top of a gun carriage so that his men could see him and follow his directions more easily. As Johnson described him, he

> made a gallant figure, . . . being dressed in a rich crimson
> [deep red] damask [a heavy, expensive patterned cloth] waist-
> coat [vest] and breeches [trousers], a red feather in his hat, a
> gold chain round his neck, with a diamond cross hanging to
> it, a sword in his hand, and two pair of pistols hanging at the
> end of a silk sling, slung over his shoulders. . . . [He] is said to
> have given his orders with boldness, and spirit.[85]

Unfortunately for his crew, Roberts's exposed position made him a perfect target. Grapeshot from the *Swallow*'s first broadside tore out his throat, killing him instantly. When one of his crewmen found him slumped over the gun carriage a few minutes later and realized that "the Great Pirate" was dead, Johnson wrote, the hardened sea rover burst into tears.

Following wishes that Roberts had often expressed, the crew threw their leader's body overboard, sword, pistols, plumed hat and all. They had very little will to fight after that. "When Roberts was gone, as tho' he had been the life and soul of the gang, their spirits sunk,"[86] Johnson wrote. By early afternoon, drenched by a fearful thunderstorm and with two of their ship's masts gone, the pirates surrendered.

Black Bart's crew gets drunk celebrating the capture of a ship, breaking his strict rules. Their drunkeness led to Black Bart's demise.

Mass Trial and Execution

The 165 white members of Roberts's crew who were still alive were put on trial at Cape Corso Castle (now in Ghana) beginning on March 28, 1722. (The Africans in the crew were sold into slavery without a trial.) All pleaded not guilty, saying that they had been forced to join Roberts's crew and had attacked other ships only under fear of death. Recognizing that this might be true for some of the men but not others, the judges agreed to hear testimony against each crew member individually.

The trials lasted a little more than three weeks. During that time the prosecution called a variety of witnesses, including men from the *Swallow* and crew members of ships that Roberts and his men had captured in Africa. The defendants were allowed to offer countertestimony if they wished. In the end, the court acquitted seventy-four pirates and found ninety-one others guilty. Of the men found guilty, two were later pardoned, seventeen were sentenced to be taken to Marshalsea Prison in England, twenty were sent to work as indentured servants (in essence, slaves) in the mines of the Royal African Company for seven years, and fifty-two of the worst offenders, including the surviving members of the House of Lords, were condemned to death and executed shortly afterward.

The capture of Bartholomew Roberts's crew resulted in the largest mass trial and execution of pirates held during the golden age. This trial was also one of the last. The times now favored the *Swallow*s of the seas instead of the *Royal Fortune*s. When "the Great Pirate" Roberts—perhaps the most successful pirate who ever lived—and his crew died, the great age of piracy died with them.

CHAPTER 8

Woodes Rogers: The Respectable Pirate

In many ways, Woodes Rogers and Bartholomew Roberts were alike. Both were excellent commanders. They knew when to be strict with those under them and when to let them have their way. Both were quiet in their personal habits, avoiding the heavy drinking, gambling, and other behavior that ruined the lives of so many of their pirate acquaintances. Both knew how to be bold, to win by bluff what they could not have taken by force. Both had a strong sense of what they wanted to accomplish and spared no effort, theirs or others', to achieve it. Both even started out in very similar activities, as attackers of ships. Under other circumstances they might have admired each other or even, perhaps, have been friends. But, although they never challenged one another directly, they came to be on opposite sides of the conflict that shook sea trade in the early 1720s: the war of the British government, its colonies, and its navy against the pirates. Roberts was "the Great Pirate," and Rogers became the greatest single destroyer of pirates.

It was no surprise that Woodes Rogers was on the respectable side of the pirate war. He was respectable from the beginning. His family came from Poole, in the part of western England called Dorset, where an ancestor had been a local sheriff and was knighted by Queen Elizabeth. Rogers's father was the captain of a ship, and he moved his family to the port city of Bristol around the time of Rogers's birth in 1679.

It was only to be expected that Rogers would go to sea as a boy and, when he became a young man, grow into a well-regarded member of the community. In 1705 he married no less than the daughter of Admiral Sir William Whetstone, commander in chief of Britain's navy in the Caribbean. Rogers and his wife, Sarah, later had three children, two daughters (one of whom died in childhood) and a son.

A Proper Privateer

Given Rogers's background and sailing experience, it was not much more of a surprise that when a group of wealthy Bristol merchants decided to sponsor a privateering venture in 1708, they asked Rogers to lead it, even though he was only twenty-nine years old. This expedition was to be as respectable as the men who bankrolled it. Unlike the earlier privateering activities of Henry Morgan, William Dampier, and William Kidd, it was completely legal. Britain was at war with Spain, whose ships Rogers attacked, during the entire time of his voyage. Only the Spanish might have called him a pirate.

Rogers hired William Dampier, then fifty-six years old, to be his pilot and navigator. The two men made a good team. Dampier knew all about winds and currents and had sailed in the Pacific Ocean, where Rogers planned to look for Spanish treasure ships. Rogers, in turn, had the ability to command that Dampier had shown so clearly that he lacked.

Rogers's two ships, the *Duke* and *Duchess,* left Bristol on August 2, 1708. He was pleased with the condition of the ships, but less so with his officers and crew of 334 men, many of whom had no sea experience. Like Dampier, he had trouble controlling them from the beginning, but unlike Dampier, he eventually succeeded in making his authority stick.

A Strange Castaway

The two ships sailed to Africa, then southwest through the Atlantic to Brazil. After that they proceeded south to round Cape Horn, the

Woodes Rogers, a respectable pirate, used the most courteous manners while robbing citizens of Guayaquil, such as these women.

stormy, icy southern tip of South America, and continued up the continent's western coast. On Dampier's advice, they planned to stop at the Juan Fernández Islands, off the coast of Chile, to careen the ships and restock their food and water. When they reached the islands in early February 1709, they were startled to see a fire blazing on the shore of the largest one, Más a Tierra.

Fearing that the Spanish might have set up an outpost on the island, Rogers sent a boat to investigate. The boat returned with a most unusual passenger: a shaggy-looking man dressed in the skins of goats, looking, Rogers wrote in his journal, "wilder than the first owners of them." [87] The man spoke English in a way that Rogers could hardly understand.

To everyone's amazement, Dampier recognized the stranger. He was Alexander Selkirk, the Scottish sailing master of the *Cinque Ports*, the smaller of the two ships on the ill-fated pri-

Castaway Alexander Selkirk stands before Rogers's crew dressed in the skins of goats.

vateering expedition that Dampier had led several years before. Selkirk explained that as the result of an argument with the *Cinque Ports*'s captain, he had been left alone on the island. He had been there ever since—four years and four months, to be exact. (He had made marks on pieces of wood to keep track of the time.) On Dampier's recommendation, Rogers made Selkirk the first mate on the *Duchess*.

The *Duke* and *Duchess* continued up the coast of South America, but they found few ships. Hoping to improve their luck, the group decided to take a leaf out of Henry Morgan's book and make a land attack. Their choice was the city of Guayaquil, then considered part of Peru but today a port in Ecuador. It was the largest ship-building center on the continent's Pacific coast. The group attacked Guayaquil on April 21, 1709, netting a haul that was decent but not outstanding.

The Manila Galleons

What the privateers really needed, Dampier insisted, was to capture one of the Manila galleons, the Spanish ships packed with valuable goods from Asia that sailed yearly from the Philippines to Mexico. The galleons were expected to pass by Baja California in December, so Rogers stationed his ships along a narrow passage in this area that the galleons would have to cross.

A few days before Christmas, the privateers spotted the ship they had been waiting for. The *Duke,* temporarily separated from the *Duchess,* took it on alone. The fighting was fearsome, but only two members of the privateer crew were injured. Unfortunately, one of them was Woodes Rogers. A shot struck him in the upper jaw, ramming pieces of jawbone down his throat and scattering blood and teeth across the deck. Shortly afterward, the Spanish ship, the *Nuestra Señora de la Encarnación Disengaño,* surrendered.

The *Encarnación* was a spectacular prize. Historian Alexander Winston writes that it "was loaded to the hatches with cloth, spices, jewels and plate [dishes and other objects made of silver and gold], thousands of ladies' fans, cotton stockings by the hundreds, [and] a set of chinaware intended for the Queen of Spain." [88] The crew of the captured ship, however, informed the privateers that this was only the smaller of the two Manila galleons sent out that year. The larger one, the *Nuestra Señora de Begoña,* had more valuable cargo still—but it was very well armed. Rogers thought that attacking such a powerful ship was unwise, but his officers' greed overruled their fear, and they in turn overruled him.

The privateers soon learned the hard way that Rogers was right. They finally spotted the *Begoña* and moved in for the attack, but the huge Spanish vessel had little trouble fighting them off. It damaged both of Rogers's ships severely, killing twenty crew members and wounding fourteen others. Rogers, who had insisted on commanding even though he was still in great pain and could hardly speak, was injured again when a shot blew away part of his left heel. He needed several weeks to recover from his wounds.

Long Journey Home

The battered *Duke* and *Duchess* now began the long journey home. Sailing by way of southern Asia, the Indian Ocean, and Africa, they eventually reached England on October 14, 1711, ending what Rogers called a "long and fatiguing voyage." [89]

According to a contemporary petition, the privateering expedition's booty was valued at eight hundred thousand English pounds.

Legal wrangles, however, delayed its distribution for five years. Dampier died before he could receive his share, and Rogers nearly went bankrupt before he finally got his.

Rogers, like Dampier before him, had kept a detailed record of his trip, and he, too, turned it into a book. The book, titled *A Cruising Voyage Round the World,* was published in 1712. Like Dampier's, it became a best-seller. It lacked Dampier's detailed descriptions of plants, animals, and native life, but it provided a lively description of an expedition at sea. Rogers's account of Alexander Selkirk, the marooned sailing master, became the basis for Daniel Defoe's famous novel *Robinson Crusoe.*

Daniel Defoe's famous novel Robinson Crusoe *is based on Rogers's account of Alexander Selkirk.*

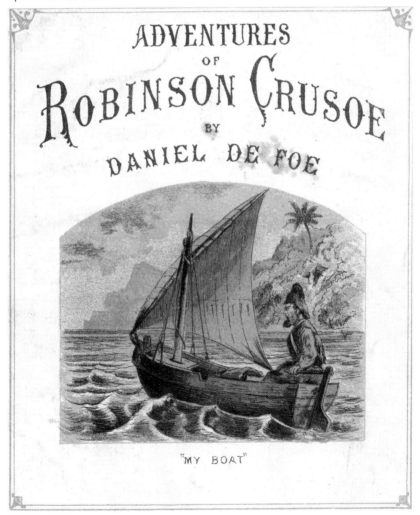

Nest of Pirates

Rogers's travels had convinced him that Britain could gain wealth and political power by establishing colonies around the world, as Spain and Holland had done. He tried to persuade backers to let him set up such a colony in Madagascar, but he could arouse no interest. He had better luck with the Bahamas, which Britain had claimed but had made no real attempt to control. These Caribbean islands' chief port, Nassau, was a notorious pirate haven, but Rogers believed he could turn the Bahamas into a profitable, law-abiding colony if he had a little help.

In 1717, Rogers persuaded the six wealthy men who leased the Bahamas from Britain to appoint him governor of the islands and send him out to take control of that "nest of pirates" [90] in any way he could. About 250 European refugees accompanied him, hoping to start farms on the islands. The British government, eager to see the pirates wiped out, threw in a hundred soldiers and the temporary services of two warships, HMS *Rose* and HMS *Milford,* as well as two smaller vessels. It authorized Rogers to offer pardons to any pirates who turned themselves in before September 5, 1718, and gave up their illegal actions.

A Spectacular Welcome

When Rogers's little fleet reached Nassau at the end of July 1718, he found only one pirate captain, Charles Vane, who wanted to challenge his authority openly. Rogers sent two of the navy ships to blockade the harbor and attempt to capture Vane. Vane, in turn, filled one of his recent prizes with flammable and explosive materials, set it on fire, and turned it loose to intercept the *Rose,* the larger of the two warships. The fire ship did no harm to the *Rose,* which backed out to sea to avoid it, but it offered the new governor an ironic welcome in the form of a spectacular fireworks display. The next day, Vane sailed out of the harbor unopposed.

The other pirates and the town's few remaining honest citizens gave Rogers a much friendlier reception. He wrote that they "show[ed] . . . many tokens of joy for the re-introduction of government," [91] though he was wise enough to suspect that not all of the joy was sincere. Most of the pirates decided to accept the British pardon, especially after they learned that Rogers planned to let them keep the booty they had already taken. Many did not really plan to reform, but some of the older sea rovers, such as Blackbeard's former teacher, Benjamin Hornigold, were ready to retire and became Rogers's staunch allies.

Struggle to Take Control

In spite of this heartening beginning, Rogers could see that he had his work cut out for him. He set about doing it as best he could. He built

Rogers built a small fort similar to the one shown here to guard the eastern entrance to the Bahamas harbor.

a small fort to guard the formerly unprotected eastern entrance to the harbor, through which Vane had escaped. He also began the more difficult task of rebuilding the half-ruined fort that guarded the main entrance to the harbor. He made Hornigold and another dependable ex-pirate his privateer commanders and sent them out to look for Vane.

Unfortunately, a disease epidemic struck Nassau a few weeks after Rogers's arrival. It wiped out would-be farmers, soldiers, and sailors alike. Fearing for their remaining crews' health, the warships' captains sailed them away. Rogers was left with almost nothing to use in keeping control of Nassau except the power of his own personality.

He knew he could not count on many of the "reformed" pirates. "Should their old friends [such as Charles Vane] have strength enough to design to attack me," he wrote in his diary, "I must doubt whether I should find one-half of the Nassau pirates to join me." [92]

Swift Justice

Rogers's biggest challenge, as it developed, came from among the island's own ex-pirates rather than from outside. In December 1718 Nassau was short of food, so he sent three ships full of ex-pirates to trade with other islands for supplies. The crews soon seized control of the ships and returned to "the sweet trade" of pirating. Furious, Rogers dispatched Ben Hornigold to catch them. Hornigold captured thirteen of the backsliders and brought them back to Nassau. Three died of wounds received in the battle, leaving ten to stand trial.

Legally, Rogers did not have the right to conduct trials for piracy. He was supposed to send such prisoners to Jamaica for trial. As a way of asserting his authority, however, he decided to try the ten pirates in Nassau instead. He formed a court with eight judges, including himself, and held the trial on December 9 and 10. Nine of the ten pirates were found guilty, and eight of them were hanged on December 12. After that, the pirate community knew one thing for certain: Whether or not Woodes Rogers succeeded in cleaning up Nassau, he was very serious about trying.

Heading Off the Spanish

Meanwhile, Rogers feared that he might soon face a different foe. He had heard rumors that war between Britain and Spain, which had ended in 1713, could begin again at any time. He knew that Nassau could not defend itself against a Spanish attack in its present condition. With cleverness worthy of Henry Morgan, Rogers used this threat to harness the energy of the restless pirates. The islanders feared a Spanish invasion as much as he did ("they'll all stand by me in case of any attempt [to attack the island] except [by] pirates," [93] he noted in his diary), so he reminded them of this danger constantly as a way of getting them to form a sort of local navy and to help him rebuild Nassau's all-important main fort. He carefully did not point out that the fort could also be used to defend the town and its harbor against pirates.

Rogers finished repairs on the fort in January 1720—just in time, as it turned out. On February 24, a fleet of Spanish ships approached Nassau harbor. Surprised to see the harbor defended, however, they held off their attack. That night they tried a Henry Morgan–style landing in small boats, hoping to invade the city by land, but Nassau's defenders spotted them and drove them off. The fleet eventually sailed away.

Neither the Spanish nor the pirates gave Woodes Rogers much trouble after that. By the end of 1720, nearly all the pirates who had formerly swarmed through Nassau had either truly reformed or moved elsewhere. Deprived of their chief land base, pirates throughout the Caribbean found "the sweet trade" much less to their liking. Although it had not completely stopped by this time, Rogers probably did more than any other single individual to end piracy in the West Indies. In his history of the golden age pirates, journalist Frank Sherry writes:

> Immensely brave, resolute, brimming over with self-assurance, Rogers always seemed to sense precisely when to take bold action—such as the hanging of the eight recalcitrants—and when to hold his peace. He knew when to bend the law to his purposes and when to ignore it. . . . He never allowed the . . . citizens of Nassau to forget that he represented the dignity, power, and majesty of England. [94]

Disastrous Debt

Rogers's success, however, came at great personal cost. Just as his earlier capture of the Manila galleon had almost ruined his health, his achievements in the Bahamas nearly ruined him financially. He had never been paid a salary and, instead, had paid most of the colony's expenses out of his own pockets. By early 1721 those pockets were almost empty. Rogers left Nassau in disgust in March, worn out with the "dangers, troubles and fatigues" [95] of his job, and sailed back to England to try to recoup some of his losses from the island's commercial and government backers. Unfortunately, no payments were forthcoming. Instead, Rogers had to declare bankruptcy and go to debtors' prison.

Rogers would not let the legal pirates defeat him any more than the illegal ones had. He called on the help of well-to-do friends, sold family properties, and pleaded his case to anyone who would listen. Finally, around 1726, his wealth and good name were restored. Respectable once more, he was appointed governor of the Bahamas for the second time in 1728. He returned to Nassau the following year, this time with a salary and his son and daughter in tow.

A Respectable End

By this time the Bahamas were also completely respectable, thriving, and free of pirates. The motto on the colony's official seal did not mention Woodes Rogers by name, but it certainly summed up his achievements: "The Pirates Expelled, Trade Restored." [96] Rogers enjoyed the respect he had so thoroughly earned until his death on July 15, 1732, at the age of fifty-four.

By the time Woodes Rogers died, pirates like the ones who had once made Nassau famous were long gone, not only from the Bahamas but also from most of the world's seas. Kidd and Bonny, Blackbeard and Black Bart, they had all followed Henry Morgan and William Dampier into history. There would be other privateers and other pirates, but none whose names would be remembered like these. Thanks to changing realities of politics and economics—and to the determination of people like Rogers—sea trade in the Caribbean and most other parts of the world had become respectable, and it would remain so.

NOTES

Chapter 1: The Pirates' Golden Age

1. Jenifer G. Marx, "Brethren of the Coast," in David Cordingly, ed., *Pirates: Terror on the High Seas—from the Caribbean to the South China Sea*. Atlanta: Turner Publishing, 1996, p. 50.

2. Quoted in David Cordingly, *Under the Black Flag: The Romance and the Reality of Life Among the Pirates*. San Diego: Harcourt Brace, 1995, pp. 192–93.

3. Quoted in Robert C. Ritchie, *Captain Kidd and the War Against the Pirates*. Cambridge, MA: Harvard University Press, 1986, p. 142.

4. Quoted in Jenifer G. Marx, "The Pirate Round," in Cordingly, ed., *Pirates*, p. 145.

5. Quoted in Charles Johnson, *A General History of the Robberies and Murders of the Most Notorious Pirates*. New York: Carroll & Graf, 1999 reprint, p. 230.

6. Cordingly, *Under the Black Flag*, p. xiv.

7. Quoted in Marcus Rediker, "Libertalia: The Pirate's Utopia," in Cordingly, ed., *Pirates*, pp. 128–29.

8. Quoted in Cordingly, *Under the Black Flag*, p. 107.

Chapter 2: Henry Morgan: The Clever Pirate

9. Alexander O. Exquemelin, *The Buccaneers of America*. Trans. Alexis Brown. 1969. Reprint, Mineola, NY: Dover Publications, 2000, p. 119.

10. Quoted in Alexander Winston, *No Man Knows My Grave: Sir Henry Morgan, Captain William Kidd, Captain Woodes Rogers in the Great Age of Privateers and Pirates, 1665–1715*. Boston: Houghton Mifflin, 1969, p. 100.

11. Exquemelin, *The Buccaneers of America*, p. 119.

12. Quoted in Cordingly, *Under the Black Flag*, p. 53.

13. Quoted in Winston, *No Man Knows My Grave*, p. 48.

14. Cordingly, *Under the Black Flag*, p. 48.

15. Exquemelin, *The Buccaneers of America*, p. 167.

16. Exquemelin, *The Buccaneers of America*, pp. 187–88.

17. Quoted in Cordingly, *Under the Black Flag*, p. 52.

18. Quoted in Patrick Pringle, *Jolly Roger: The Story of the Great Age of Piracy.* New York: W.W. Norton, 1953, p. 77.

19. Quoted in Winston, *No Man Knows My Grave,* p. 86.

20. Quoted in Winston, *No Man Knows My Grave,* p. 89.

21. Quoted in Winston, *No Man Knows My Grave,* p. 94.

22. Quoted in Winston, *No Man Knows My Grave,* p. 105.

Chapter 3: William Dampier: The Explorer Pirate

23. Quoted in Christopher Lloyd, *William Dampier.* Hamden, CT: Archon Books, 1966, p. 16.

24. Quoted in Lloyd, *William Dampier,* p. 15.

25. Quoted in Lloyd, *William Dampier,* p. 28.

26. Quoted in Lloyd, *William Dampier,* p. 12.

27. Quoted in Lloyd, *William Dampier,* p. 56.

28. Quoted in Simon Craig, "No Ordinary Man," *Geographical Magazine,* March 1998, p. 65.

29. Quoted in Lloyd, *William Dampier,* p. 39.

30. Lloyd, *William Dampier,* p. 30.

31. Craig, "No Ordinary Man," p. 65.

32. Quoted in Craig, "No Ordinary Man," p. 67.

33. Quoted in Lloyd, *William Dampier,* p. 97.

34. Quoted in Lloyd, *William Dampier,* p. 99.

35. *Athena Review,* "The New World Voyages of William Dampier." (www.athenapub.com/damp1.htm.)

36. Quoted in Cordingly, *Under the Black Flag,* p. 85.

Chapter 4: William Kidd: The Unlucky Pirate

37. Quoted in Ritchie, *Captain Kidd and the War Against the Pirates,* p. 31.

38. Ritchie, *Captain Kidd and the War Against the Pirates,* p. 94.

39. Quoted in Ritchie, *Captain Kidd and the War Against the Pirates,* p. 106.

40. Quoted in Ritchie, *Captain Kidd and the War Against the Pirates,* p. 106.

41. Quoted in Ritchie, *Captain Kidd and the War Against the Pirates,* p. 106.

42. Quoted in Ritchie, *Captain Kidd and the War Against the Pirates,* p. 116.

43. Quoted in Marx, "The Pirate Round," in Cordingly, ed., *Pirates,* p. 159.

44. Quoted in Ritchie, *Captain Kidd and the War Against the Pirates,* p. 192.

45. Quoted in Cordingly, *Under the Black Flag,* p. 180.

46. Quoted in Frank Sherry, *Raiders and Rebels: The Golden Age of Piracy.* New York: Hearst Marine Books, 1986, p. 190.

47. Quoted in Sherry, *Raiders and Rebels,* p. 190.

48. Quoted in Ritchie, *Captain Kidd and the War Against the Pirates,* p. 220.

Chapter 5: Edward Teach (Blackbeard): The Fearsome Pirate

49. Johnson, *General History,* p. 70.

50. Johnson, *General History,* p. 55.

51. Johnson, *General History,* p. 67.

52. Johnson, *General History,* p. 69.

53. Sherry, *Raiders and Rebels,* p. 241.

54. Sherry, *Raiders and Rebels,* p. 245.

55. Quoted in Robert E. Lee, *Blackbeard the Pirate: A Reappraisal of His Life and Times.* Winston-Salem, NC: John F. Blair, 1974, p. 107.

56. Quoted in Johnson, *General History,* p. 65.

57. Quoted in Johnson, *General History,* p. 66.

58. Johnson, *General History,* p. 71.

59. Pringle, *Jolly Roger,* p. 209.

Chapter 6: Anne Bonny: The Woman Pirate

60. Johnson, *General History,* p. 130.

61. Johnson, *General History,* p. 143.

62. Cordingly, *Under the Black Flag,* p. 57.

63. Johnson, *General History,* p. 132.

64. Cordingly, *Under the Black Flag,* p. 67.

65. Johnson, *General History,* p. 134.

66. Johnson, *General History*, p. 144.

67. Quoted in Tamara J. Eastman and Constance Bond, *The Pirate Trial of Anne Bonny and Mary Read*. Cambria Pines by the Sea, CA: Fern Canyon Press, 2000, p. 52.

68. Quoted in Eastman and Bond, *Pirate Trial of Bonny and Read*, p. 55.

69. Quoted in Eastman and Bond, *Pirate Trial of Bonny and Read*, p. 54.

70. Quoted in Jenifer G. Marx, "The Golden Age of Piracy," in Cordingly, ed., *Pirates*, p. 118.

Chapter 7: Bartholomew Roberts: The Successful Pirate

71. Quoted in Johnson, *General History*, p. 230.

72. Cordingly, *Under the Black Flag*, p. 110.

73. Johnson, *General History*, p. 230.

74. Quoted in Johnson, *General History*, p. 176.

75. Johnson, *General History*, p. 176.

76. Pringle, *Jolly Roger*, p. 237.

77. Johnson, *General History*, p. 198.

78. Johnson, *General History*, p. 198.

79. Johnson, *General History*, p. 198.

80. Johnson, *General History*, p. 201.

81. Quoted in Sherry, *Raiders and Rebels*, p. 330.

82. Johnson, *General History*, p. 204.

83. Stanley Richards, *Black Bart*. Llandybie, Carmarthenshire, Wales: Christopher Davies, 1966, p. 59.

84. Quoted in Johnson, *General History*, p. 260.

85. Johnson, *General History*, p. 229.

86. Johnson, *General History*, p. 231.

Chapter 8: Woodes Rogers: The Respectable Pirate

87. Quoted in Cordingly, *Under the Black Flag*, p. 140.

88. Winston, *No Man Knows My Grave*, p. 208.

89. Quoted in Winston, *No Man Knows My Grave*, p. 213.

90. Quoted in Cordingly, *Under the Black Flag*, p. 151.

91. Quoted in Cordingly, *Under the Black Flag*, p. 153.

92. Quoted in Sherry, *Raiders and Rebels*, p. 255.

93. Quoted in Sherry, *Raiders and Rebels*, p. 255.

94. Sherry, *Raiders and Rebels*, p. 278.

95. Quoted in Winston, *No Man Knows My Grave*, p. 217.

96. Quoted in Sherry, *Raiders and Rebels*, p. 358.

FOR FURTHER READING

Books

David Cordingly, *Under the Black Flag: The Romance and the Reality of Life Among the Pirates*. San Diego: Harcourt Brace, 1995. Authoritative and interesting account of pirate life by a former curator of the National Maritime Museum in Greenwich, England.

Stephen Currie, *World History: Pirates*. San Diego: Lucent Books, 2001. Account of pirates and their effects on world history, for young adults.

Charles Johnson, *A General History of the Robberies and Murders of the Most Notorious Pirates*. New York: Carroll & Graf, 1999 reprint. Lively, partly fictionalized contemporary account of famous British and American pirates, possibly written by Daniel Defoe.

Stuart A. Kallen, *The Way People Live: Life Among the Pirates*. San Diego: Lucent Books, 1999. For young adults. Describes daily life among modern pirates as well as pirates of the golden age; separates history from myths.

Angus Konstam, *The History of Pirates*. New York: Lyons Press, 1999. Well-illustrated overview of pirate history and famous pirates.

Albert Marrin, *Terror of the Spanish Main: Sir Henry Morgan and His Buccaneers*. New York: Dutton, 1999. Slightly fictionalized account of Morgan's life and his raids on Spanish cities. For young adults.

Jan Rogozinski, *Pirates! An A–Z Encyclopedia*. New York: Facts On File, 1995. Encyclopedia includes articles on pirate books and movies as well as biographies of historical pirates and information on special subjects such as ships and use of torture.

Myra Weatherly, *Women Pirates: Eight Stories of Adventure*. Greensboro, NC: Morgan Reynolds, 1998. Covers women pirates from a variety of periods, including Anne Bonny and Mary Read, Chinese pirate Cheng I Sao, and Irish pirate Grace O'Malley. For young adults.

Periodicals

Constance Bond, "A Fury from Hell—or Was He?" *Smithsonian*, February 2000.

Richard Cavendish, "Execution of Captain Kidd," *History Today*, May 2001.

Alec Foege, "Sunken Dream," *People Weekly*, May 22, 2000.

Bob Graham, "Blackbeard Rises Again," *American Archaeology*, Fall 1998.

Websites

Beej's Pirate Image Archive (www.ecst.csuchico.edu/~beej/pirates). Pictures of famous pirates, battles, ships, and more, as well as links and further reading.

Robert H. Ossian, Pirates' Cove (www.geocities.com/Athens/7012/main. html). Includes short biographies of famous pirates and other useful information about pirate history.

Pirates: An Educational Website Devoted to the Subject of Piracy (www.piratesinfo.com/main.html). Distinguishes between facts and legends about pirates and provides resources, bibliography, and other useful information for students.

Rochdale State School, Pirates (www.rochedalss.qld.edu.au/pirates). Well-designed website provides brief biographies of famous pirates, pictures of pirates, and other resources for students.

WORKS CONSULTED

Books

David Cordingly, ed., *Pirates: Terror on the High Seas—from the Caribbean to the South China Sea*. Atlanta: Turner Publishing, 1996. Well-illustrated anthology of articles by experts on pirates, covering such topics as buccaneers, the golden age of piracy, and the Pirate Round.

Tamara J. Eastman and Constance Bond, *The Pirate Trial of Anne Bonny and Mary Read*. Cambria Pines by the Sea, CA: Fern Canyon Press, 2000. Provides background information on golden age pirates, biographical information on Bonny and Read (including some original research), and a transcript of their trial.

Alexander O. Exquemelin, *The Buccaneers of America*. Trans. Alexis Brown. 1969. Reprint, Mineola, NY: Dover Publications, 2000. Contemporary account of daily life of the buccaneers and Henry Morgan's raids on Spanish cities by a man who accompanied the buccaneers as a surgeon.

Robert E. Lee, *Blackbeard the Pirate: A Reappraisal of His Life and Times*. Winston-Salem, NC: John F. Blair, 1974. Biography of Blackbeard includes background material on political and economic factors affecting people's opinions of him and information about related trials.

Christopher Lloyd, *William Dampier*. Hamden, CT: Archon Books, 1966. Biography of Dampier, stressing his skill as a writer, natural scientist, and navigator.

John Masefield, ed., *Dampier's Voyages*. London: E. Grant Richards, 1906. Includes *A New Voyage Round the World*, *A Voyage to New Holland*, and other writings by Dampier, as well as an introduction and biographical sketch by Britain's poet laureate.

Patrick Pringle, *Jolly Roger: The Story of the Great Age of Piracy*. New York: W.W. Norton, 1953. Account of the golden age of piracy and the famous pirates who lived during that time.

Stanley Richards, *Black Bart*. Llandybie, Carmarthenshire, Wales: Christopher Davies, 1966. Biography of Bartholomew Roberts, probably the most successful pirate of the Golden Age.

Robert C. Ritchie, *Captain Kidd and the War Against the Pirates*. Cambridge, MA: Harvard University Press, 1986. Biography of William Kidd includes extensive information on political and economic factors that affected his rise and fall, and on life in the pirate settlements around Madagascar in the 1690s.

Frank Sherry, *Raiders and Rebels: The Golden Age of Piracy.* New York: Hearst Marine Books, 1986. Lively account of the golden age pirates includes extensive historical and biographical information.

Alexander Winston, *No Man Knows My Grave: Sir Henry Morgan, Captain William Kidd, Captain Woodes Rogers in the Great Age of Privateers and Pirates, 1665–1715.* Boston: Houghton Mifflin, 1969. Biographies of three of the most important privateers of the golden age.

Periodicals

Athena Review, "The New World Voyages of William Dampier." www.athenapub.com/damp1.htm.

Simon Craig, "No Ordinary Man," *Geographical Magazine,* March 1998.

Bruce Heydt, "William Kidd's Last Voyage," *British History,* May 1996.

The Islander, "Roebuck Wreck Found," March 22, 2001. www.the-islander.org.ac/1528.htm.

Elliot Kriegsman, "In Search of Blackbeard," *Historic Traveler,* 1997. www.thehistorynet.com/historictraveler/articles/1997/1097_text.htm.

Randall Silvis, "A Hell of Our Own: The Nether World of Blackbeard," *Destination Discovery,* May 1993.

George Humphrey Yetter, "When Blackbeard Scourged the Seas," *Colonial Williamsburg Journal,* Autumn 1992.

Internet Sources

Randy Bieland, "Pirate Ghosts," Discovery Channel, 1998. www.discovery.com/stories/history/pirates/pirates.html.

"Blackbeard's Home Page," Ocracoke Island, NC, www.ocracoke-nc.com/blackbeard.

"Blackbeard the Pirate . . . and the Presumed Wreck of the *Queen Anne's Revenge,*" North Carolina Maritime Museum, 2001. www.ah.dcr.state.nc.us/sections/maritime/blackbeard/default.htm.

Franco's Cybertemple, "The Life and Times of Sir Henry Morgan." www.cavazzi.com/morgan.

Paul Hawkins, "Captain Kidd's Island Found," 2000. www.pfrh.supanet.com.

David D. Moore, "A General History of Blackbeard the Pirate, the *Queen Anne's Revenge and the Adventure,*" North Carolina Division of Archives and History, 1999. www.ah.dcr.state.nc.us/qar/HISTORY/history1.htm.

Paul Perry, "Diving for Captain Kidd's Sunken Ship," Discovery Channel, January 29, 2000. www.discovery.com/exp/madagascar/captainkidd/dispatch.html.

Julie Ann Powers, "Blackbeard's Flagship?" CoastalGuide/ICW-Net. www.coastalguide.com/nc/seagrant/seagrant01.htm.

"Sir Henry Morgan." www.mesa.k12.co.us/pirates/morgan.html.

"Sir Henry Morgan: The Pirate's Pirate." www.angelfire.com/pa2/Panama2Hot/morgan.html.

"Welcome to the North Carolina Home of Blackbeard the Pirate!" Beaufort, North Carolina, 2001. www.blackbeardthepirate.com.

John Weston, "Sir Henry Morgan, 1635–1688: A Brief Note of His Career," Data Wales, 2000. www.data-wales.co.uk/morgan.htm.

INDEX

Admiralty Board, 52
Africa, 74–77
Arawaks, 10
archaeology, 23
Ascension Island, 41
Australia, 37, 38–42

Bahamas, 13, 68, 90–94
Barnett, Jonathan, 71
Bellamy, 23
Bellomont, Earl of, 46, 51, 55
Black Bart
  African expeditions of, 74–77,
    80–84
  on benefits of pirate life, 16
  birth and childhood of, 74
  boldness of, 77–78
  Dampier and, 86–89
  death of, 82–83
  flag of, 74
  leadership and, 43–44, 77,
    78–79
  New England raids of,
    78–79
  nickname source, 74
  personal qualities of, 79, 85
  rules of, 79
  success of, 74
  trial and punishments of
    crews of, 84
  see also ships
Blackbeard
  birth and childhood, 57
  Charleston blockade and, 60
  death of, 65
  description of, 56
  Honduras and, 59
  Jamaica and, 58
  last battle of, 63–65

  marriage of, 61
  reputation of, 56, 58, 59–60
  tactics of, 56
  see also ships
Board of Trade, 32
Bonnet, Stede, 59, 61
Bonny, Anne
  birth and childhood of, 67–68
  capture of, 72
  legends about, 73
  marriage of, 68
  reputation of, 68
  trial of, 72–73
booty. *See* cargoes; treasure
Brazil, 77–78
British East India Company, 47,
  51
buccaneers, 10
  see also pirates
Buccaneers of America, The
  (Exquemelin), 22
buccans (Caribbean grills), 10
Burney, James, 44

Calico Jack, 68–73
cargoes, 13–14, 78
  see also treasure
Chagre River, 30
Charles II (king of England),
  32–33
Charleston, South Carolina, 60,
  68
Chile, 87
Cook, James, 40, 44
Coote, Richard. *See* Bellomont,
  Earl of
Cordingly, David, 17, 27, 68,
  70, 74
Craig, Simon, 39

PICTURE CREDITS

About the Author

Lisa Yount earned a bachelor's degree with honors in English and creative writing from Stanford University. She has been a professional writer for more than thirty years, producing educational materials, magazine articles, and more than thirty books and anthologies for young adults and adults. She usually writes about biology and medicine but also enjoys writing biographies of adventurous people such as pirates. Her books for Lucent include *History Makers: Disease Detectives*. She lives in El Cerrito, California, with her husband, Harry Henderson, a large library, and several cats.